Lincoln's Administration

Selected Essays by
Gideon Welles

Lincoln's Administration

Compiled by
ALBERT MORDELL

TWAYNE PUBLISHERS
New York

PREFACE

This second volume of selected essays by Gideon Welles contains the remainder of the articles written for *The Galaxy* and the *Atlantic Monthly* by Lincoln's Secretary of the Navy. Although they were originally published in nine different instalments between 1876 and 1878, these essays dealt with only three major topics: the nomination and election of Abraham Lincoln, the administration of Abraham Lincoln, and the election of 1864. Like their predecessors, they constitute a coherent account which sheds much light on the politics of the Civil War and reconstruction.

As he did in his earlier essays, Welles again emphasized his main thesis: the greatness of Abraham Lincoln. As the author put it, the Civil War President "was in many respects a remarkable man, never while living fully understood or appreciated." Determined to correct any remaining misconceptions about the Great Emancipator, the former Secretary of the Navy succeeded admirably in delineating his chief's political sagacity. How Lincoln rose to power, how he managed to maintain a middle course against opponents both within and outside of his party, and how he laid the foundations for a mild policy of restoration— these are the high points of the essays. Since he sympathized with the President during the struggle over reconstruction, Welles sought to prove that Andrew Johnson was merely trying to carry out his predecessor's plans. To the author, it was clear that Johnson's antagonists had opposed Lincoln long before the end of the war. Consequently, Welles tended to stress the difficulties between Lincoln and the radicals, men whom he considered as dangerous as the Democratic opposition. Although his strictures upon the extremists were probably influenced by his difficulties with them during reconstruction, his views were widely accepted by historians in later years.

If Welles disliked radicals such as Benjamin F. Wade, Thaddeus Stevens, and Edwin M. Stanton, he also heartily disapproved of General Grant. When General Richard Taylor, in an article in the *North American Review*, stated that Abraham Lincoln and not Ulysses S. Grant was responsible for the costly overland march upon Richmond in 1864, Welles believed it imperative to repel the charge. Repel it he did. Carefully marshalling his facts, in these articles he proved conclusively Grant's responsibility for the details of the 1864 campaign and absolved Lincoln from blame. Later historical research has borne him out.

Taken in conjunction with Howard K. Beale's new edition of *The Diary of Gideon Welles*, the articles collected in these two volumes constitute a valuable source for the study of the Civil War. Mr. Mordell has earned the gratitude of all those interested in the conflict for compiling the essays at this time. Their reappearance should prove a boon for laymen and professionals alike.

H. L. Trefousse

Staten Island, New York
January, 1960

CONTENTS

INTRODUCTION

In the preceding volume of uncollected articles by Gideon Welles, *Civil War and Reconstruction,* there were two on Lincoln, "Lincoln and Johnson" and "The History of Emancipation." The present volume has the other uncollected essays that Welles wrote.

It is fortunate that Welles wrote these articles on Lincoln for *The Galaxy* and the *Atlantic Monthly.* He was the only member of Lincoln's cabinet who devoted himself so much to writing about Lincoln. He depicted in a masterly fashion the struggles Lincoln encountered not only in his own party but outside of it, and convincingly emphasized the superb statesmanship that Lincoln displayed. With few exceptions, Welles agreed with Lincoln in all his policies. These articles deserve applause from the South, for he stood by Lincoln and Johnson in extending amnesty to all those engaged in the secession cause. He presented a strong case against the so-called radicals, who wanted to treat the southern states harshly as conquered provinces and even to confiscate the property of southerners. The leaders against this policy—H. W. Davis, B. F. Wade, Thaddeus Stevens and Charles Sumner—had the support of a large part of the Congress and succeeded in imposing a military rule over the South, a form of reconstruction that has left a bitter taste to this day.

As Welles shows, what was uncanny in Lincoln was his sense of timing; Lincoln knew when to act on matters of which he first disapproved. Welles shows that Lincoln was not only a great, humane person, but that at the same time he was an astute constitutional lawyer, faithfully interpreting the Constitution in maintaining a conciliatory attitude towards the South. Welles shrewdly observes that Johnson was impeached and nearly convicted for following Lincoln's policy.

At this time, no further Lincoln eulogies are necessary. We have also been made familiar with the hostile attacks upon him by various parties and groups, by orators and newspapers, prior to the election of 1864. Nevertheless, after his assassination, great animosity was expressed against him by Democrats and radicals.

No doubt the reader will be surprised with the numerous instances in which General Grant, as a military commander, comes under Welles's fire, and also by the emphasis laid on the fact that it was he, Welles, and not Grant who instigated the important attack upon Fort Fisher.

Welles had written in his *Diary*, August 30, 1864, as follows: "I have been urging a conjoint attack upon Wilmington for months. . . . The War Department hangs fire and the President whilst agreeing with me, dislikes to press the matters when the military leaders are reluctant to move." This, I would assume, means Grant himself was opposed to the expedition.

After the first attack on Fort Fisher failed, Welles, upon receiving the report of Admiral D. D. Porter, noted in his *Diary*, December 31, 1864, that he had sent a telegram to Grant (this contained an invitation for his military co-operation) and that Grant answered that he would comply with Welles's request.

A passage in Grant's *Memoirs* says that he *"determined* [italics supplied] with the concurrence of the Navy Department in December, to send an expedition against Fort Fisher for the purpose of capturing it." Comparing this with the telegram that Grant had sent in answer to Welles's for co-operation, we see that he was carrying out orders, for Stanton acted as a go-between. He had not "determined"; he merely complied in carrying out Welles's idea.

In making this statement, Grant should probably be absolved from an attempt at deliberate deception. At this time he knew that he was dying from cancer, and we may admire him more for his heroism than condemn him for what might have been a slip of memory.

Welles is supported by Captain O. Selfridge in his claim for originating the idea of sending the expedition. The Captain took part in the attack. In his article "The Navy at Fort Fisher" in *Battles and Leaders of the Civil War* he says, "When the Secretary of the Navy, Mr. Welles, recognizing the importance of closing the port of Wilmington, urged upon President Lincoln to direct a co-operation of the army, General Grant was requested

to supply the necessary force from the troops about Richmond."
Selfridge also corroborates Welles in saying that for the purposes
of the second attack, Welles again sought the co-operation of the
army, to which Grant at once acceded.

I should like to conclude with the citation of a personal
account by one who took part in the assault and who related
to me his part. I published this in the *Evening Bulletin,* October
23, 1929. William Dugan was a gunner on the *Wabash,* a ship
on which he served with George Dewey before the Civil War, on
a cruise in the Mediterranean. I wrote as follows: "He [Dugan]
was of the party that landed in the second attack on Fort Fisher.
In Dugan's opinion, it was a mistake to have sailors who were
only armed with cutlasses and revolvers make up the attacking
party.* Naturally, many of the men were wounded and the attack
itself was not altogether at first successful . . . Dugan had
charge of a division in both attacks. . . . He said, 'It was an interesting spectacle, guns recoiling and every man bent on doing
his duty.' " Incidentally, he said Admiral Porter was not popular.

Thus Welles is sustained in the claim that he made that he
and not Grant was the originator of the important expedition to
Fort Fisher which virtually closed the war and in holding that
the navy was deprived of credit for its share in the attack, even
though the final assault was made by the army.

ALBERT MORDELL

---

* This is borne out by Daniel Ammen, also a participant in both attacks,
in his book *The Atlantic Coast.* He said, "The cutlasses and revolvers in
the hands of the sailors were quite inoperative." He told of his experiences
in that masterly autobiography, *The Old Navy and the New.*

1

Nomination and Election of Abraham Lincoln

ACCOUNT OF HIS ADMINISTRATION

In this essay, Gideon Welles, the former Jacksonian
Democrat, presents his view of the background of the
twenty-five years leading up to the Civil War. His
strictures upon Henry Clay as well as upon John C.
Calhoun attest to the constancy of his admiration for
the principles of Old Hickory and explain many of
his actions during and after the Great Rebellion.

PART ONE

THE NOMINATION of Abraham Lincoln in 1860 was an
unexpected event to the active party politicians of the period.
Men of all parties, previous to the session of the convention at
Chicago, supposed that the delegates were to assemble and per-
form a prearranged part. Several names were, it is true, suggested
as competitors, but only one of them seemed formidable, and the
first ballot taken demonstrated that his supporters were more
numerous and better prepared and disciplined than the others.

The result, so different from general expectation, proved that
the convention, while it disappointed almost all of the mere
party men who take upon themselves the management and
direction of these irresponsible nominating conventions, was on
that occasion fortunate in its selection of a candidate. It has not
always been the case that these party gatherings, which are
convened for the purpose of forestalling the legitimate and legal

The Galaxy, XXII (September, 1876).

13

operation of the Constitution, have been as judicious in their
selection as the convention at Chicago in 1860. Indeed, this
process of making a President, to which parties have for some
years resorted, is demoralizing in its effects and calculated to
elevate small men who are intriguers, or who have active
intriguing friends, over the best intellects and highest statesmanship of the country. It moreover tends beyond any scheme
yet devised to the overthrow of State individuality and State
action, by which our Federal system is likely to be undermined
and the government ultimately centralized and consolidated.
Every fourth year the people are stimulated and aroused from
one end of the country to the other, by public meetings and by
the press, and are excited in almost every conceivable way to
defeat State action and centralize the country on some aspiring
individual for the office of President in a way different from
the prescribed constitutional method. Contentions, alienations,
strife, and bitterness are kindled. Delegates, many of them of
exceptionable character and unworthy of confidence, men, some
of whom are willing to be bribed, and if bribed cannot be
punished, are chosen by persons no better than themselves to
assemble in conventions and dictate to the people whom they
they shall vote for and elect to be their Chief Magistrate. The
framers of the Constitution, anticipating many of these difficulties, and aware also of the dangers that attend embittered contested popular national elections under ambitious and unscrupulous leaders, endeavored to place the choice of Chief Magistrate
remote from public commotion and angry controversy by intermediate and contingent agencies. The Constitution as originally
framed provided that each State shall appoint a number of
electors equal to the whole number of Senators and Representatives to which the State may be entitled. These electors, so
appointed, were to meet in their respective States and vote for
two persons, etc. The phraseology is peculiar. The President,
Vice-President, Senators, and members of Congress must be
chosen or *elected* to their respective offices, but electors of
President and Vice-President are to be *appointed*. "No Senator
or Representative, etc., shall be *appointed* an elector." Two
Senators shall be *chosen* by the Legislature," etc. Members of

the House of Representatives "shall be *chosen* every second year by the people."

It was obviously the intention of the framers of the Constitution that the electors should be appointed, not chosen or elected by a popular vote. They were in fact appointed by the Legislature of most of the States in the early years of the government. The Legislature of each State was to direct in what manner electors should be appointed—whether by a concurrent vote or a joint vote of the Legislature, or by the Governor and Council, or otherwise, the Constitution did not prescribe—that was reserved to the States respectively. It was clearly not to be a popular election. The electors appointed were to meet, not collectively at the seat of government or at any central point, but in their respective States, and to cast their votes for two persons for President and Vice-President. They were not, however, to concentrate or specify which of the two should be preferred, but one at least of the persons voted for shall not be an inhabitant of the same State with themselves.

This machinery to make a President, it will be remembered, was before the days of modern telegraphs or railroads; and as all the electors appointed were to vote in their respective States on the same day, it was believed that concert, centralization, combination, personal strifes, or any extensive national controversy would be obviated. Men of mature age and character, in whose judgment and intelligence the public had confidence, would, it was expected, be appointed; and the electors, possessing patriotism, integrity, and candid judgment that would lead them to discuss the subject dispassionately when they met in the States, would vote for two men, one of whom might be a local favorite, but one at least would be qualified to administer the government. It was not expected that any one after General Washington, on whom all were united in the first instance, would be likely to receive the required constitutional majority, and be chosen by the vote of the electors in their colleges. In that event the electoral vote would be merely a nomination. The Representatives in Congress would then, voting by States, each State to cast one vote, select from the five persons who received the highest number of electoral votes the individual who should be President. By this process a number of statesmen, five at least, would come before the country. It was anticipated that not only the excitement and madness attending a popular election of the Executive or Chief Magistrate would be avoided, but the federal principle of State equality would be preserved and enforced in the final determination, when there was non-agreement of a majority of the electors. Unfortunately for the successful working of this carefully elaborated plan, there was in the violently contested Presidential election of 1800 such unity among the Republican opponents of the Adams administration, that there was a tie between Jefferson and Burr, who had each an equal number of votes and a majority over their competitors; but neither of the two principle candidates received a higher vote than the other. Every elector who voted for them, whether *appointed* by the Legislature or *chosen* by the people, intended Jefferson should be President. Under these circumstances the defeated party, who had voted for other candidates, and were against both Jefferson and Burr claimed that the choice of the republic was for Burr; and as by the Constitution Congress was in the event of a tie vote to decide between them, an exasperated and almost revolutionary proceeding took place. This unhappy intrigue and abuse of power, which threatened for a time the national tranquillity, led to a change, called an amendment of the Constitution, by which the political fabric that had been so carefully and elaborately constructed in 1787 was broken down. Congressional caucuses and irresponsible national conventions, the hotbeds of party and personal intrigue, were substituted. The federal principle of political equality of the States, essential to State individuality and the distinctive rights and sovereignty of the small States, in the event of no choice by the electors—one of the great compromises in the formation of the Constitution—has been undermined. Consolidation and centralization, which override the principles that led to the Union, have in practice become a popular doctrine, and irresponsible gatherings, called conventions, composed to a great extent of active party men and intriguing partisan politicians who make politics a trade, virtually dictate to the country who shall be the Chief Magistrate and first officer in the republic.

Men of little experience, and with very slight qualfications for civil service, but who for that reason are considered more available than statesmen of undoubted ability and well known public service, are often selected by their irresponsible conventions, and no alternative is left the people but to vote for one or the other of the inferior persons so designated.

The electors themselves are no longer permitted to vote for two individuals for President and thereby prevent the public mind from concentrating on one ambitious aspirant; but under the amendment of 1804 they "shall name in their ballots the person voted for as President," and should there be no choice, Congress shall select from the three highest instead of from the *five* highest candidates. It is a curious fact that this amendment, which insidiously saps the federal principle and tends to consolidation, was introduced and adopted by the party opposed to centralization, and who were *par excellence* the advocates of States' rights. A perversion and abuse of constitutional power by a defeated and excited minority was the moving cause for this amendment or change of the organic law, which has been followed by combinations and illegitimate proceedings, where active intrigues have prevailed in the election of Presidents. The electors now are mere dummies, intermediate agents, allowed no judgment or discretion, but are pledged instruments to vote for such persons as the illegitimate nominating convention dictates. It is worthy of consideration whether it would not be an improvement, under the change that was made in 1804, and the usage that has followed, were the people to vote direct for President and Vice-President.

The nomination of Mr. Lincoln was, as has been remarked, a general disappointment to active politicians. Partisans in each of the old political organizations, expecting a different selection before the result was announced had prepared themselves for the conflict—one for attack, the other for defence—in the confident belief that William H. Seward would be the Republican candidate. The managing party politicians of New York, who to a great extent controlled the Republicans of that State by a profligate system of legislative grants, bounties, and favors, possessed themselves of a large amount of funds to secure the success of their favorite; and their scarcely less objectionable opponents in Washington and elsewhere, not doubting that the Albany candidate would be the Republican nominee, shaped their tactics accordingly. In consequence of the unexpected turn of affairs at the Republican National Convention, the machinery of the old parties was thrown out of gearing, and some heavy political guns were spiked or exploded without effect.

The overthrow of an administration and of a dominant party and its policy after a severe contest must be almost inevitably a strain upon the government, and will doubtless in the future as in the past be productive of consequences more or less painful to the country. A sweeping removal of incumbents, especially of those who are non-partisan, but who are familiar with their duties and the usages and traditions of the government, attended by the introduction of inexperienced men in their places, must cause more or less derangement, and devolve greatly increased labor on the principals or heads of departments, who are held responsible for the faithful and successful administration of affairs.

Mr. Lincoln was elected by a large majority of the electoral votes, in conformity with all the requirements of the Constitution, but was in a minority. The Democratic party, which had for years wielded the government, and was still all-powerful in numbers, had become factious, demoralized, and divided on questions sectional in their character, and which to some extent violated fundamental principles. The newly formed Republican organization was composed of persons not entirely homogeneous in political principles and opinions, but they were on the exciting questions of the day united in action. Another party, distinct from both the great organizations, styling itself American, or Know-Nothing, made up of incongruous elements, but with candidates of recognized intelligence and ability, received a considerable support.

Mr. Lincoln's election was in a great measure the result of Democratic dissensions which had their origin in a misuse and abuse of power, and in a departure from those professed principles of strict adherence to the Constitution and regard for the Union and reserved sovereignty of the States which had given that party vitality and strength. Immediately after the election, and months before Mr. Lincoln entered upon his duties or had performed any official act whatever, the restless politicians of South Carolina—oligarchs in principle—who claimed for their feeble State absolute sovereignty, commenced a revolutionary career, and their disunion example was followed by other States, claiming the "inalienable right to abolish the existing government" and to establish a new one, which in the utopian and imaginary excess of party they fancied might be more acceptable than that to which they belonged and owed allegiance.

During the winter of 1860-61 these seceding or sectional States were active in organizing and preparing for a conflict with the national authority, while the Federal Government, thus threatened, supinely submitted to the seizure of forts, arsenals, and the public property in the seceding States. It was claimed that the right to resist the general Government and destroy the Union was "inalienable," but that for the Government to assert its authority, maintain its integrity and the unity of the national property in the seceding States, was an exercise of arbitrary and tyrannical power which could not be acquiesced in or permitted. The outgoing Executive declared that a State could not be coerced. Consequently treason or infidelity to the Federal Government must go unpunished, but disobedience to the State which resisted the national authority should be attended with confiscation and death. Congress, while it did not endorse or assent to the theory of the President, manifested a strange apathy or indifference to the impending storm, and adopted no measures to recover and hold the public property illegally seized, or to vindicate the national authority, but whiled away the winter of 1861 in factious controversy scarcely less reprehensible than Executive imbecility.

It is not necessary to discuss in this place the political doctrinal points of that period, when fidelity to party seemed with a large portion of the community more binding and more sacred than constitutional obligations, and when obedience to the mandates of a State whose authorities were in flagrant rebellion, defying and resisting the national Government in its exercise of rightful, legal, delegated, and constitutional power, was en-

forced by local law. Whatever may have been the real views of
the leaders of secession, there is no doubt a large portion of
their followers and adherents entertained the belief that in the
event of a collision between the State and national Governments
it was their duty to obey the State without regard to the merits of
the controversy of the legality of its enactments. Doubt and confusion prevailed among the masses of the people in consequence
of the divided or double allegiance which all owed to the State
and Federal Governments. The powers of the States being primi-
tive and those of the Federal Government derivative—the latter
being created by the States, which had relinquished and delegated to the general Government certain specified powers that are
indispensably necessary to the welfare of all—gave to the malcontents apparent justification for the assumption that any State
which became discontented had a right to resume for itself the
powers which, with others, it had granted away for the common
benefit and general welfare. Without discriminating as to the
condition and rightful authority of each, the secessionists claimed
that any one of the States could resume and exercise the
rights which had been conceded to the general Government,
though to resume that authority would be destructive of the
general Government and of the national Federal Union. While
these were the doctrines of one class of extremists, the centralists,
on the other extreme, then and subsequently, claimed for the
Federal Government absolute authority over the States, insisted
that it could divide them and create new States by such division,
could enlarge or diminish State jurisdiction, and deny States
representation in either branch of Congress. One class asserted
the right to secede and leave the Union; the other maintained
authority in the central Government to exclude or to expel
States from the Union and deprive them of their constitutional
and reserved original rights.

It was in the midst of these conflicting opinions, but the
results of either then not fully developed or understood, that
Mr. Lincoln reached Washington and was inaugurated. His position was in every respect not only of the gravest responsibility,
but of extreme delicacy and embarrassment. He had been elected

according to the prescribed forms of the Constitution as amended, but was chosen by a minority of the people. Preliminary steps for a dissolution of the Union and the overthrow of the government had already been taken in one section of the country. The retiring administration had witnessed with meek submission the seizure of forts, arsenals, and custom-houses by the insurrectionists, declaring amid the falling ruins its inability to coerce a State and thus preserve the national integrity. The Thirty-sixth Congress, with almost equal imbecility, beheld with apparent indifference this disintegration and threatened downfall of the civil fabric, and adjourned without any effective legislative preparation for the impending conflict. The republic was rent by factions. A large section was in open rebellion; another bordering and sympathizing section south of the Potomac and the Ohio stood in a defiant attitude, declaring if the Federal Government attempted to enforce its authority by supplying or reinforcing the garrisons, or by taking possession of the national property in the seceding States, it would be considered a tyrannical, aggressive, and arbitrary exercise of power; an attempt at coercion and subjugation which would justify and call for united resistance. On his journey to Washington to enter upon the labors of government, the President elect was warned by his selected Secretary of State, and by the General-in-Chief of the army, that his way through Baltimore was beset with assassins. To avoid and defeat them, Mr. Lincoln, against his own opinion, was persuaded by these advisers, and others who were associated with them and in their confidence, to pass through that city *incog.* and in advance of the train which had been prescribed in the programme of his journey. The hegira from Harrisburg, and his unexpected arrival in Washington twenty-four hours in advance of the specified time, were the cause of much surprise and no little regret to his friends, and of sneers and ridicule on the part of his opponents. This extraordinary but perhaps necessary proceeding was planned by Mr. Seward and General Scott, whose suspicions had been excited by the detectives in their employ. Subsequent events in Baltimore gave some confirmation to apprehen-

sions which were censured at the time as a mere contrivance
to alarm the President elect, and place him under obligations
to one of his chosen counsellors.

The difficulties which confronted the President on the day
of his inauguration, and which the Administration encountered
daily and hourly in the spring of 1861, were never fully appreciated nor rightly understood. They were only known and
felt by the actors on whom at that momentous period devolved
the responsibility of government, most of whom were called
from retirement or seclusion into the public service under the
most extraordinary circumstances which ever took place in
human experience. A majority of the people had voted against
or had declined to vote for Mr. Lincoln, and were still unwilling to give him their support. Nearly one-half, under the
discipline of party, were determined not to acquiesce in his
policy or measures, whatever they might be. The country under-
went not only a change of administration but of parties, carrying
in its train the overthrow and downfall of a long established
dynasty, which for a series of years had shaped the course of the
government and directed public affairs. But the crisis involved
more than a mere change of men, or a revolution of parties.
There was a sectional combination which designedly improved
the occasion to effect the subversion of the government and a
dismemberment of the Federal Union. The very danger apprehended by the framers of the Constitution from excited national
parties, which, deaf to patriotism, would enlist the passions and
animosities of the whole people in a popular election, had
occurred. The founders of the government had, as already mentioned, foreseen and sought to avoid such national disturbance
in the choice of Chief Magistrate by a federal system, first in
the *appointment* of electors on a federal basis by the separate
action of the States, and in the event of no one receiving a
majority of the electoral vote, a choice was to be effected by
the Representatives in Congress, voting by States, all of them
equal in sovereignty and political rights, each State of the
Union to have by their Representatives in Congress one vote.
But this carefully prepared political machinery had been in-
terrupted and broken down, first, by *choosing* the electors

by the people instead of *appointing* them in such manner as the Legislature of each State might direct; and secondly, by the amendment of the Constitution in 1804, adopted in consequence of an attempted fraud by violent partisans in the election of 1801, when the defeated party sought to supersede Jefferson by electing Burr. Congressional caucuses and national conventions intervened thereafter to prevent legal constitutional action. Irresponsible delegates of opposing factions gathered in these national assemblages and selected candidates under the organization and discipline of party; no alternative remained for the people but to vote for electors pledged to one or the other of the candidates thus designated.

Mr. Lincoln was confronted at the beginning of his administration by a large majority who had voted for others in preference to him. There would have been a majority in Congress to oppose any extreme views had he possessed them, provided the Senators and Representatives from the cotton States had remained at their post. But to have remained would not have been secession. A brief trial would, the leaders well knew, have satisfied the people that the foreboding and threatened evils which were pronounced against black Republican rule were not wholly imaginative and false; hence a dissolution by secession or withdrawal from the Union before the new administration was fairly launched, became necessary to consummate the schemes of the chiefs in the great conspiracy.

No cause whatever existed for breaking up the government. The pretext at the beginning of sectional strife had been that there were higher duties on imports than were necessary, and that laws were enacted to protect certain industries and monopolies, rather than to raise a revenue by internal taxation; these alleged grievances were declared so offensive, the burden so great and so unequal in its operation that John C. Calhoun and his disciples felt themselves compelled to throw off the load which they pronounced intolerable and insupportable, first by an attempt to nullify the federal laws. Defeated in the nullification movement, the same discontented spirits resorted to another; they soon and without cause professed great alarm for the institution of slavery, which they represented to be in jeopardy from the preaching and theories of abolitionists, and all in the free States were denounced as abolitionists. This was an appeal calculated and intended to excite alarm and rouse the feelings of all interested in slave property; yet so groundless was the pretext that more than a quarter of a century of unceasing declamatory assertion and violent denunciation and invective were requisite for the consummation of the disunion conspiracy. Professing ultra States' rights and anti-central principles, these sectional leaders, nevertheless, insisted that slavery was national, not local; that the institution demanded central protection, and must have from the general Government additional guarantees for its preservation and perpetuation. While clamorous to be let alone and permitted to have their own way, they invoked federal power and federal legislation in behalf of slavery, which was not national and which existed only by permission of the States. Mr. Lincoln and his friends denied that slavery was the offspring or creature of the republic, maintained that it was local and belonged to the States respectively where it was authorized, and that those States could not and should not be interfered with, but that they should be let alone to enjoy or reject it without interference or molestation by the central Government.

Party contentions had on repeated occasions, in both the State and general governments, been carried to extreme lengths on the subject of slavery, from an early period. For forty years this controversy, agitated and discussed by humanitarians on one hand and the advocates of slavery on the other, had been fostered by ambitious party leaders. When in 1820 and again in 1850 Congress and the public mind had become embittered and inflamed so as to almost threaten the public tranquillity, Henry Clay, a popular party leader, at the critical culminating moment came forward with a proposition to *compromise* the subject in dispute, and thus allay the storm which he had contributed as much as and perhaps more than any one to raise. His success in repeatedly effecting a peaceable if not always satisfactory or beneficent adjustment of this and other questions, had procured for him the name of the "Great Compromiser," which partisan adherents were delighted to bestow on him as their political chief. From 1820 to 1850 he had been the aspiring but unsuccessful chief of a party, formidable from its wealth and numbers, which favored central power; and his frequent plans of compromise, often in derogation of the Constitution were by many supposed his highest claims and best qualifications for the office of President. The long political training which the country had experienced and his friends followed under the tutelage of this distinguished legislator, begat a policy of temporizing expedients, often by a sacrifice of principle, which was not always useful or productive of the happiest results. But the fame of the "Great Compromiser" stimulated others of easy political virtue, seeking notoriety, and who were not strongly wedded to principle, to imitate this eloquent leader.

During the winter of 1861 numerous imitators of Mr. Clay appeared with schemes and propositions to compromise existing difficulties—most of them temporizing and unworthy—by concessions to the seceders, and with devices to conciliate and satisfy those who were determined not to be satisfied. Some of these compromises were by proposed amendments to the Constitution; others, not to be restrained by the organic law, advocated extraordinary and unwarranted legislation, and all by a sacrifice of principle. The authors of these propositions, apprehensive of disaster by a rigid adherence to the Constitution, were generally sincere and patriotic, if not always profound, wise, or sagacious, in their schemes. Many of their associates, less sincere, professed a readiness and anxiety to effect a compromise, but were by no means earnest, if they were not actually indifferent or opposed to any arrangement. A majority of Congress, embracing men of both parties, opposed any legislative action. The secessionists on their part really wanted and were determined on disunion; others, opposed to them, were convinced that no legal measure or legitimate legislation would satisfy the faction which for thirty years had labored to break up the Union and overthrow the government. Under these circumstances the Thirty-sixth Congress closed its term and adjourned without doing anything toward reconciliation, by peaceable or other means, and without any preparatory legislation or the adoption of any measures to strengthen the incoming administration in any effort it might make to preserve the national integrity.

Political party organizations then as in after years, more than constitutional obligations, controlled Congress. Party discipline had created an antagonism in States where there was really little difference of principle; but such was in the influence of association and the discipline and imperious exaction of party, that thousands excused and defended the doctrine of secession who had no intention of favoring national dismemberment. Mingled with this partyism, and soon a part of it, was sectional animosity, which contributed to generate a hostile feeling toward States and people whose industries were different. The right of secession had been agitated by aspiring and theoretical politicians, and discussed in promiscuous gatherings and in the political papers by men who in early stages of the discussion had little or no idea that secession would ever be put in practice, or that to effect it there would be a resort to arms. Gradually, however, the doctrine became a familiar topic, and at length began to be seriously and favorably entertained, not only in South Carolina, where an oligarchy entertained and cherished extreme views, but the political party managers in States South, particularly those on the Gulf, adopted the disorganizing and revolutionary doctrine that secession was a reserved right. Politicians and party conventions in the cotton States busied themselves for years in inculcating the right of secession, and were tolerated and listened to by the people without any expectation of a resort to extreme measures, and therefore without serious rebuke; but after long training, with labored design, the disunionists made advances, and finally obtained control of the local State governments.

On the election of Lincoln the leaders proceeded to put their revolutionary schemes in operation, and were recognized and upheld by the governments of those States. Until then the great body of the people in the States South had been passive disbelievers in and were opposed to disunion. They had witnessed and participated in political party controversies apparently as violent; had for thirty years heard from the party teachers of the nullifying school empty threats of resistance to Federal authority and denunciations of the Federal Government as tyrannical, arbitrary, and oppressive; all of which excitements had passed off in peaceful adjustments of every real or alleged grievance. They were willing to believe that such would be the ultimate termination of the secession agitation; but the secessionists had in the mean time, by persevering, persistent assiduity, succeeded in securing possession of the civil administration of nearly every State south of the Potomac. When, therefore, Mr. Lincoln commenced his administration, the governments of these States were arrayed against him, and one-half of them against all Federal authority. In those States which had not already passed ordinances of secession, the active, calculating, and leading politicians were in avowed sympathy with the secessionists, and those citizens who rejected the doctrine and still adhered to the Union and maintained the supremacy of the Federal Government did so at their peril. They were denounced as traitors to the State, to which it was imperiously asserted they owed first and the highest allegiance. All in the insurrectionary States who persisted in supporting the Union and the Federal Government, after the passage of the ordinance or secession by their State, were subject to be proceeded against as traitors, their property to be confiscated, and they and their families imprisoned and punished. Between the upper and nether millstone of the Federal and State Governments the citizen was brought in jeopardy, and as the action of the State was more prompt and decisive than of the national Government, no choice was left the citizen but unconditional submission to the usurping State government, if he regarded the welfare of his family and the preservation of his property, which was doomed to confiscation if he continued a faithful, adhering citizen of the United States. Under the usurped, radical, and revolutionary ordinances and decrees of the seceding States, and the neglect of the general Government submission to the arbitrary local decrees and enactments was the only alternative left to the resident citizen. The same citizen, thus coerced and compelled to submit, against his wish, will, and conviction, to the dictation of the State, was a few years later, after the rebellion was suppressed, disfranchised by a fragmentary Congress and denied the right of representation in the national Government. If true to the Union, he was pronounced a traitor to the State; if he submitted to and obeyed the laws of the State, he was treated as guilty of treason by Congress, which assumed to exercise both executive and legislative powers.

2

Nomination and Election of Abraham Lincoln

ACCOUNT OF HIS ADMINISTRATION

The opening days of the Lincoln administration were the most difficult ever experienced by any American government. The secession of the Southern states, the relief of Fort Sumter, the insubordination of Secretary of State William H. Seward, and the importunities of swarms of office seekers—all these problems confronted the new President. How he solved them in his own manner and established his unchallenged supremacy in the administration is here recounted by his Secretary of the Navy.

PART TWO

AT THE TIME of Mr. Lincoln's inauguration, the actual existing status and the future of the people—unionists and secessionists—to what extent the law would be resisted on one hand or enforced on the other, were uncertain, indefinite, and unknown. Multitudes, a majority without doubt through the whole of the States South, with perhaps the exception of South Carolina, who had from party considerations or from sincere apprehensions opposed the election of Mr. Lincoln, acquiesced, though disappointed in the result, and were ready to support his administration; but they were not permitted to do this by the leaders who had possession of the seceding State governments. The President, though well aware of the mischievous intent of the prominent persons in this conspiracy, was reluctant to believe they would resort to armed resistance, and

The Galaxy, XXII (October, 1876).

entered upon his duties with the kindest and most tolerant feelings toward all, whether friends or opponents of his election.

But party spirit had been moved to excess, and became virulent. Extreme partisans in the free States stimulated and encouraged discontent, and were scarcely less malignant in their feelings than the secessionists. In the slave States the positive element overpowered the mild, passive, and peaceably disposed friends of the Union and of social order, who deprecated and shrank from violence. The patriotic citizens knew that there was no cause for rebellion or revolution, and, relying on the Federal Government, as in the days of Jackson, for protection against rebels, were comparatively quiet and inert. Bold measures and a decisive and energetic policy on the part of the Federal Government, especially the Executive, at the commencement, such as had been displayed by Jackson in the days of nullification, were necessary for their security, and would at the same time have aroused them to duty and to action.

The executive power of the Government is by the Constitution vested in the President; and to pretermit or disregard the legal and necessary exercise of this power thus delegated to him may be as culpable, and in an emergency may be a greater wrong to the country than the assumption or usurpation of undelegated authority, to preserve the national integrity. Mr. Buchanan had been an intelligent Senator, but was inherently a timid and always a calculating politician, sensitive as regarded his party standing, in consequence of early political equivocations, and was undoubtedly more obedient to party requirements from that circumstance. Intending to do what was about right, but usually relying more on the opinion of his associates than his own convictions—always cautious and irresolute when there was responsibility—he was in those closing days of his administration, with broken and divided counsels, feeble, irresolute, vacillating, and almost imbecile of purpose. Most of his cabinet advisers were unfaithful. The forts of the South were neglected, most of them were without garrisons, and there was stationed in none of the discontented States a military force properly commanded, to sustain the Government and enforce the laws, or to form a nucleus around which the patriotic citi-

zens could rally to maintain the national supremacy against
the seceding State governments. The Federal troops, instead of
being stationed where they could render efficient service, had
been sent, under Twiggs, a traitor and a renegade, to western
Texas, or to territories still more remote, from which or from
Texas they could not be speedily recalled. The Southern mari-
time frontier was in scarcely better condition. The commanders
of the navy yards at Pensacola and Norfolk, the only naval stations in the Southern States, were old and inefficient officers,
who, if not unfaithful themselves, were surrounded by energetic
subordinates that were in sympathy with the secessionists, and
ultimately proved faithless. Most of the sailors and naval vessels
in commission were on foreign stations. Those which constituted
what was called the "home squadron" were in the West Indies
or the Gulf of Mexico, about as inaccessible and remote from
immediate communication, except through the insurrectionary
region, as the squadron in the Mediterranean. The treasury
was empty, and the national credit had been impaired by the
conduct of Cobb, the seceding Secretary, who, until he retired,
had charge of the finances. On the change of administration the
government was, in all its departments in a dilapidated and
deranged condition, which had been evidently designed by those
who had in view a dissolution of the Union.

In the construction of his Cabinet, some of the characteristics
of Mr. Lincoln, and the purpose by which he was to be governed
in his administration, were developed. New issues had given
birth to a new political organization. Old parties had become
dismembered and broken into factions. The Democrats were
divided, and had presented the previous fall two candidates—
Breckenridge and Douglas—for the Presidency. Douglas received
and was the undoubted choice of a large majority of his party.
He had, however, but few votes from his old opponents. Breckenridge had among his supporters such of the dismembered
Whig element of the South as did not give their votes to John
Bell, the "Know-Nothing" candidate. If there were men at the
South in favor of Mr. Lincoln, or who had a preference for the
Republican party and principles, such was the prevailing prej-
udice and intolerance in that section that no full ticket of

electors was permitted to appear. No press was allowed to advocate Lincoln's election, and to express an opinion favorable
to either Republican principles or the Republican candidates
was attended with no inconsiderable personal peril. The factious
and fragmentary condition of the Democratic party, and the
violent sectional hostility of the South toward Republicans, had
the effect of strengthening and uniting the new party, composed
of both Whigs and Democrats, in the free States, and secured for
Mr. Lincoln the electoral vote of each and all of them except
New Jersey.

Mr. Lincoln was well aware that it was no old and beaten path
which he was to travel in administering the government, with veteran associates who had been lifelong political friends engaged in
an organization for the same cause, but that without precedents
to guide, an untrodden course lay before him, requiring an
entirely new and different departure from that which had been
pursued by either of his predecessors. Not only was he to establish an administration differing in many respects from theirs, and
to consolidate a new organization, but he was to do this with
materials which, in political principles, had been discordant and
antagonistic in the past. These previously opposing elements he
was to reconcile and bring into harmonious action, and at the
same time encounter a violent and unsparing opposition. Quietly, without ostentation, and at the same time without just offence to any, or submission to professed and intrusive advice
and influence, voluntarily tendered and pressed upon him, he
selected for his constitutional advisers persons who, in their
antecedents, had politically been opposed, but who were nevertheless representative men of the various elements which elected
him, and constituted at his inauguration the Republican party.
In his choice of counsellors he kept in view the original purpose
of consolidating these elements into one great united party,
which would sustain his administration, and ultimately embrace
all who desired to maintain the Constitution and the Union.
This purpose, distinctly and honestly avowed, led him to invite
his own rival Republican competitors to participate in the administration, and also induced him to associate in his Cabinet
men of differing political antecedents. Such a policy, however,

did not comport with the views and wishes of some of his friends, who, in the overthrow of the Democrats, had anticipated a Whig triumph rather than Republican success. The pressure upon him in that regard, with a view of reviving the Whig party, was for a time very great; but while he patiently listened and calmly discussed the subject, no argument or appeals caused him to change his original purpose of a Republican administration, without identification with past or committal to current controversies or either of the old political organizations.

The individuals composing his Cabinet had but slight previous personal intimacy with Mr. Lincoln, or with each other. There was no concerted or combined effort among the members themselves, or by their respective friends, to influence the President in selecting his advisers, with the exception, perhaps of a few managing politicians in New York and Pennsylvania. A very strenuous and persistent effort was made by certain partisans in New York, who had been Whigs, to exclude Mr. Chase, and also to prevent the appointment of either Mr. Blair or Mr. Welles.

In the nominating convention at Chicago Mr. Seward had been the chief competitor with Mr. Lincoln, and being also a well known politician and statesman, holding at the time the position of Senator from the State of New York, it was not only desired by his friends, but supposed and generally expected, that he would be offered the State Department. It was intimated by some of his confidential friends that while the tender of this place was due as a matter of courtesy to Mr. Seward, that gentleman would probably decline accepting the office. In that event it was the intention of Mr. Lincoln, who knew not with what sincerity these doubts of the Senator's acceptance were made, to have invited Mr. Chase to be his Secretary of State. Otherwise the latter gentleman was invited to administer the finances. There was on the part of both Mr. Seward and Mr. Chase coyness as to accepting a seat in the Cabinet, which, as regarded the former, was more affected than sincere. Mr. Chase may have honestly hesitated to take the second position, for he was very ambitious, and had just been a second time elected to represent Ohio for six years in the Senate, and his taste, studies, and abilities were unquestionably better adapted to legislative than purely financial service. While, therefore, he could not have hesitated for a moment to go into the State Department, he was not, with his personal aspirations, so ready to relinquish his senatorial term of six years in order to accept a seat in the Cabinet subject to the pleasure of the President for its continuance, and which, moreover, placed him, while entering upon duties with which he was not familiar, in a position inferior in public estimation to that of his rival political competitor.

On the great questions which were pending, and which then divided the country, these two gentleman were not in strict accord. Mr. Seward, less tenacious of principle, and more pliable in his nature, had expressed a willingness to yield his opinions on the slavery question, and to so revise the Constitution as to make it conform to the demands of the secessionists. Mr. Chase, on the contrary, was opposed to any concession or compromise which should commit the national Government to the cause or to the perpetuation of slavery beyond the limits prescribed in the Constitution. Mr. Lincoln was well aware of the differences between these two officers—differences which extended to his supporters—but did not deem it expedient that he should in the then turbulent and excited period commit himself and his administration to either, beyond what was enunciated in his inaugural address. Personally he was opposed to slavery, but being a constitutionalist, he was as decidedly opposed to the schemes of the abolitionists, and determined, while administering the Federal Government, to abstain from any interference with the local law on this subject, or any of the reserved rights of the States. He had strong hopes that the exciting disunion question would, when his views and intentions were understood, pass away without a serious conflict, and was confirmed in these hopes by the assurances of his selected Secretary of State. Mr. Seward, sanguine by nature, fruitful in expedients, and willing to make concessions, was confident of a speedy restoration of amicable feelings after the change of administration; and his position and opportunities had been such as to inspire his colleagues as well as the President with a hope that his predictions were not unfounded. Subsequent events proved that these prophetic declarations and assurances, if not baseless, were mere delusions, predicated on no substantial fact or principle, but mere imaginary anticipations of what he would be able to accomplish by expedients. His assurances, if founded on any concert with his opponents, may be taken as an exhibition of his readiness to acquiesce in almost any change of the fundamental law itself to get over a temporary difficulty.

There had been, as the President and his Cabinet were advised, some understanding and concert between Mr. Seward and leading secessionists, as well as with a portion of Mr. Buchanan's Cabinet, from which important results were expected after the 4th of March. What sincerity there may have been on the part of the secessionists with whom he held converse, and what were their expectations, other than an absolute acquiescence in their demands, which the declarations of Mr. Seward in his January speech, and his action and proceedings for several weeks subsequent to the accession of Mr. Lincoln, and his official despatch to Mr. Adams seem to indicate, may never be fully known. Mr. Edwin M. Stanton, the Attorney-General of Mr. Buchanan, had during the closing months of the Buchanan administration secretly informed Mr. Seward of the proceedings and purposes of the administration of which he was a part; and from these several sources of communication Mr. Seward persuaded himself that he held the key to all discontent, and that when once in place he could reconcile disagreements and lock up all disturbance. Without knowing precisely how his Secretary of State was to restore harmony, Mr. Lincoln trusted at the beginning to the reputation of Mr. Seward for intelligence, sagacity, and ability to accomplish what was prophesied and promised. It was this almost implicit trust in Mr. Seward at the commencement which for a time caused serious embarrassment, and almost forfeited the confidence of the country in the ability and integrity of the President to administer the government.

Mr. Chase, though an avowed anti-slavery man, was solicitous that it should be understood he was not an abolitionist, nor connected with that organization. The schemes

for compromise, especially such as involved a change of the
Constitution in behalf of slavery, or committed the Government to the support or perpetuation of human bondage in
any form, beyond the compromises already made, he strenuously opposed. But he was possessed of unappeasable ambition for official power and distinction; not that he desired
power for personal aggrandizement, but from a belief that
he could in position do more than others for his country and
for freedom. But the discussions in the winter of 1861, the ex-
citable and persistent determination of the authorities of South
Carolina and the Gulf States to throw off Federal allegiance,
with the readiness of Mr. Seward to "meet exaction with concession," and an expressed willingness to change the Constitution
in fundamental particulars to conciliate the secessionists, were
incidents not without their influence on the course of Mr.
Chase. While he would not consent or be a party to a change
of the Constitution in behalf of slavery, he became impressed
with doubts and misgivings, from what he heard and witnessed
of the emphatic determination of the secession leaders, and from
the countenance and support given them by the Democrats in
the free States, from the yielding disposition of Mr. Seward, Mr.
Crittenden, and other Republicans and friends of the new administration, who were willing to compromise and even to reconstruct the government in order to preserve the national territorial integrity, whether the Union of the States could be
maintained. Reconciliation he considered impossible. Civil War
he deprecated, and the way to extricate the country from its
embarrassment and sustain the Government was, he confessed,
dark and inexplicable. I was pained beyond measure, or my
ability to express, when, retiring one morning from a Cabinet
consultation, he made known to me his doubts and misgivings,
and that he had come to the conclusion it was best that the
States which desired to leave the Union should be permitted
to go without hindrance. It was not to be denied, he said, that
our government was not one of force, yet it was manifest the
Union could not be maintained except by compulsion, and a
compulsory Union would be no Union, but war, contention, a
despotic exercise of power. In what could this and would

this terminate, but an utter subversion of our system and of republican government?

It was near the last of the month of March that he thus opened his mind to me. He probably had not at that time communicated his views or speculations to any other person. He certainly had made no such intimations in any of the Cabinet consultations. We had left the executive mansion together that morning after a pretty earnest and anxious discussion of the condition of affairs and the threatened difficulties, without any satisfactory conclusion; but it was obvious that Mr. Seward had taken even a more advanced step in that direction than Mr. Chase, and was prepared to surrender Sumter and other forts in the seceding States to the local authorities, to call a national convention to revise the Constitution and reconstruct the government. The attitude of Mr. Seward caused me little surprise; for it was well understood by those who knew him that he was an optimist, governed less by convictions and fixed laws than by expedients, and that he had more faith in his skill and management to govern and accomplish a purpose than in the Constitution or any political principle; but the suggestions of Mr. Chase, who was at the time greatly depressed and discouraged, astounded and shocked me. I so expressed myself. He said secession, in his opinion, would be no permanent alienation; the seceding States would, after a brief experience, be satisfied that the benefits of the Union greatly exceeded any real or fancied grievance, and they would themselves soon ask to be again admitted. My views were that the Union, when once broken, like shattered glass, could never again be made whole. I so expressed myself in one or two interviews which immediately followed. With the hurried and momentous events that were shortly precipitated upon the country, his doubts were dissipated, his confidence in the Union was strengthened, and the duty and necessity of putting forth the whole power and energy of the Administration to preserve it never thereafter faltered.

On these points the other members of the Cabinet were a unit, firm and unswerving for the Union, though one or two of them were reported to have favored the Crittenden compro-

mise. Mr. Blair, who resided in Washington, and was familiar
with the men, and had watched the schemes of the disunionists,
was wholly opposed to any temporizing, and to all proposed
expedients which abandoned old landmarks. From the first
he insisted that the Administration would be delinquent if it
failed to exercise promptly and energetically the power with
which it was invested to suppress insurrection and every attempt at resistance to the government and laws. The greater
the delay, and the longer the Administration hesitated, the
more serious would be the consequences to the country. His
position was antagonistic to that of Mr. Seward from the commencement; and he never, as did Mr. Chase, doubted.

The President listened to the views and suggestions of each
and all, but wisely forbore to hastily commit himself. What he
wished was, first of all, delay until the Administration could
get in working order, so that the whole country should be
aware of his intention to administer the government faithfully,
without prejudice or sectional partiality. With prudent sagacity
he cautiously pursued his way, carefully observing and weighing
the views of each of his counsellors, and every suggestion made,
vigilantly watching events, and feeling the public pulse.

The repeal of the Missouri compromise had caused great irri-
tation. He inquired whether, in the opinion of the Cabinet,
a restoration of that compromise would serve to allay excitement, but received no favorable response. He, and many others
doubtless, attached greater importance to that unwise and injudicious proceeding than it merited. The repeal of the compromise was an impolitic act, which had undoubtedly greatly
aggravated the prevailing discontent; but it was one of the
incidents, not the primary cause of sectional contention. It was
stated that while the repeal was uncalled for and injudicious,
after the long acquiescence of the country in the enactment, its
restoration would not promote harmony, for the compromise
was, in itself, a violation of the principles on which our federal
structure was founded; that it created sectional distinction; had
generated sectionalism by permitting and professing to give legal
sanction to favored residents south of a particular parallel of

latitude, by conferring on them certain rights and the exercise of certain powers which were denied to all residing north of that parallel; that the Federal Government was not authorized to make such distinction; that equality of political rights to all of the States was a dogma or fundamental principle of our government; that among the grants of power specified in the Constitution there was none which authorized Congress to establish slavery, yet by the Missouri compromise act Congress had assumed the power to establish or permit it south of the latitude 36 deg. 30 min., and to exclude it north of that line. If slavery was a privilege or right, those above as well as those below the line were entitled to it; for all sections and States were to be treated alike. If it was not a privilege or right, Congress had committed a great wrong in authorizing or attempting to authorize it. Had Congress done its duty faithfully in 1820, instead of compromising and evading it, we should have been spared present evils, and it did not become the Administration to sanction and attempt to reëstablish a palpable wrong.

Whatever expedients, schemes, or ideas of compromise any members of the Government may have entertained or projected to satisfy the disunionists, none were adopted, and the policy of Mr. Lincoln was to adhere to the Constitution and observe its requirements and restrictions, without innovations or any change of the organic law, to appease factions. This was of course unsatisfactory to the secessionists, who claimed that these States had already withdrawn from the Union and established a separate government.

On the day of his inauguration Mr. Lincoln received through President Buchanan information from Major Anderson, in command of Fort Sumter, that the supplies of his garrison would be exhausted in six weeks. On the succeeding day commissioners from the confederacy of the insurrectionary States arrived in Washington, and soon after requested of the Secretary of State that a day might be named when they could present their credentials to President Lincoln. An answer was, by concert or understanding between the commissioners and Mr. Seward, delayed for a month. In the meantime the affairs of the govern-

ment and country, which, with the changes of administration and
a new order of things, had been in something of a chaotic condition, were in a degree arranged.

While overwhelmed by the disorders and disturbances growing out of the insurrection, the Administration was also beset
on every hand to make almost universal and indiscriminate
party changes of the Federal officers. The President and some
of the Cabinet, particularly the Secretary of State, were disposed
to go beyond others in these respects. It was claimed, on one
hand, that only Democrats held Federal appointments, but it
was said on the other hand that many of these were Union
men, opposed to secession, who in their devotion to country had
risen above mere party, and that it would be politic and wise
to make a distinction between them and those extreme partisans
who were secessionists, or sympathizers with the secessionists;
that while, from the very long continuance of Democrats in
power, most of the office-holders were of that party, it was
evident that in the departments, especially bureau officers and
clerks who were faithful and familiar with their duties and
knew the acts and traditions of the government and the departments to which they were attached, should be retained, unless they were disunionists or politically offensive, whatever
were their private opinions on political questions. Many ardent
and extreme party men who were secessionists had, on the change
of administration or immediately after, resigned their places.
This was particularly the case in the Navy Department, where
there was great political demoralization. The voluntary withdrawal of these men, which it was supposed would embarrass
the Secretary, in fact relieved him of the necessity of removing
many subordinates. Some who remained were not exempt from
suspicions, and perhaps one or two from association and social
intercourse were infected with the prevailing secession epidemic,
but only one, it is believed, proved treacherous or false; nor is
it certain that he was guilty of any act of infidelity. In the
Navy Department, therefore, nothing of what is called proscription for opinion's sake was exercised; and what was done was
in so quiet a manner, was acknowledged to be so just, and in
such contrast with some others, that a clamor was raised against

the Secretary for his forbearance. Exceptions had been taken by men who had been ultra Whigs to his appointment as one of the President's advisers, on account of his Democratic antecedents, and it was intimated that his opposition to sweeping and indiscriminate removals by the Administration, and the omission on his part to make changes, was in consequence of old political partialities.

The fact was that extensive removals in his department were unnecessary, for the vacancies created could not be immediately filled by competent persons, in whose ability and fidelity he, in the general break-up, had confidence. Nevertheless, after considerable pressure, and statements of what other heads of departments had done, it was proposed, in order to appease the grumblers, that at least one change should be made in each of the navy bureaus and one in the department proper. This would, it was said, prevent invidious distinction, comparisons, and complaints, as regarded the other departments, and contribute to consolidate and make uniform the policy of the Administration. There was a species of refined political or party casuistry in this, which it was unnecessary to controvert; but as the Secretary knew not the views and opinions of each and all the subordinates with whom he had recently been brought in contact, he preferred that the removals thus ordered should be received and considered as an act of the Administration rather than of the department, and therefore devolved on his chiefs the duty of designating which clerks under the rule should be dismissed. While the Secretary of the Navy declined to remove persons from office who were faithful to the government and true to the Union, whatever had been their party antecedents, some others took a different view, and discharged, with little discrimination, such as were Democrats, regardless of their capacity, experience, fitness, or fidelity. It was this difference which led the President, who wished uniform policy and action, to make the request or order for the removal of a few clerks in the Navy Department. There were not many civil appointments at the disposal of the Secretary of the Navy, and these were connected with the navy yards. Most of these were then, as now, under the vicious system of putting party electioneerers in

place, violent partisans. Such were promptly dismissed. It was
justly felt that none but reliable and trusty Union men should
in the then existing difficulties be retained in positions of responsibility. For years it had been the policy of successful administrations to make sweeping changes of opponents. In the peculiar condition of the country it seemed wise to conciliate and
retain such as were patriotic and well disposed, though some
opposed it. The President was compelled to face the responsibility and act on these and other questions. In striving to
reconcile and bring into united action opposing views, he was
accused of wasting his time in a great emergency on mere party
appointments. Under the pressure and influences that were
brought to bear upon him, particularly by members of Congress,
who should never be permitted to dictate appointments, some
things were doubtless done which, under other circumstances,
and left to himself, he would have ordered differently. Extensive
removals and appointments were, in the general disorder, not
only expected, but absolutely necessary, beyond previous experience, yet never under any administration were greater care
and deliberation required. A host of ravenous partisans from
Maine to California—a large proportion of them Whigs long
excluded from office, but who had participated in the election
of Mr. Lincoln—filled Washington, and, backed by their Senators and Representatives, besieged the White House and departments, demanding for themselves or their friends the local appointments, regardless of the patriotism or real merits of the
incumbents. This crowd of active friends, with their importunities, at such a crisis, was of course embarrassing to the new
Administration, which commenced its labors with a demoralized
government and crumbling Union that needed the vigilant attention of the wisest and most considerate statesmanship for
its preservation. Not until the adjournment of the Senate,
which held an extra session as usual on the change of administration, was there any let-up on the subject of removals from
office.

In the mean time the Administration was not remiss in attention to the condition of the country and the disordered state
of public affairs. Some members of the Government were con-

fident that the hostilities of a serious character would be avoided—all hoped such might be the case; but there were others who believed a conflict more or less serious was inevitable. The President, though a patient listener to the views and suggestions of others, was nevertheless a keen and attentive observer of all that was said and done, and promised to be done, but he came to no hasty conclusion. His final decision for the relief of Fort Sumter, the most important and immediate question pending, was postponed until the supplies of the garrison were nearly exhausted. To the last moment he and his Cabinet indulged the hope that peace would be preserved; but the insurrection had proceeded to such lengths that it was not doubted resistance to collecting the revenue would be attempted. In this he was confirmed by General Scott, to whose opinion he early paid great deference, and General Scott, remembering the old nullification conflict under Jackson, apprehended and hoped that the culminating point would be, not in reinforcing Sumter, but in the enforced collection of duties on imports. In fact, both General Scott and Mr. Seward, acting in concert, advised and expected the evacuation of Sumter, which would throw the responsibilities of a collision on the treasury and the navy instead of the military, for the navy would be called upon to sustain the treasury in collecting the duties. Sumter would, in compliance with the advice, and wishes and views of the Secretary of State and the General-in-Chief, be abandoned. It was at this juncture, and while the determination in regard to Sumter was yet unannounced, that the President, desirous of ascertaining his own strength and that the Administration should know the actual condition of the navy without exciting suspicion as to his purpose, addressed to me the following note:

EXECUTIVE MANSION, March 18, 1861.

Sir: I shall be obliged if you will inform me what amount of naval force you could at once place at the control of the revenue service. And also, whether at some distance of time you could so place an additional force, and how much? and at what time? Your obedient servant,

A. LINCOLN.

Hon. Secretary of the Navy.

To this I, on the 20th, gave him an answer in detail, stating the condition and position of every naval vessel, whether in or out of commission, and the actual personal force employed or authorized by law to be employed, together with an estimate of the time necessary to fit out the vessels which were in ordinary, and to recall the squadrons that were on foreign stations. The letter of Mr. Lincoln was written fourteen days after his inauguration, and twelve days after the Cabinet was installed. It makes no allusion to Forts Sumter or Pickens, nor to any naval or military operations, offensive or defensive. There was extensive espionage, and every movement of the Administration was watched. If any who favored or expected the evacuation of Sumter and Pickens should see the correspondence, their suspicions would not be stimulated by the information asked and given in reply to an order calling for a statement of the naval force, and how much could be placed at the "control of the revenue service." It was essential that the President should be in possession of the exact condition of the navy should it be necessary to enforce the collection of the revenue. Had he called for a statement direct without reference to the revenue, or had the Secretary of the Navy presented it without explanation, suspicion would in the then sensitive condition of the public mind in regard to Sumter have been aroused. This would have been particularly the case with those who expected or had given assurance or encouragement that the fort would be evacuated. Besides the Secretary of State and the General-in-Chief, who advocated and had taken for granted that the fort would be surrendered, there were other officials in high position, some of whom soon abandoned the Government, that were in sympathy with the secessionists, but at the time this order was given were watching and waiting events. An attempt to collect the revenue did not alarm them; an order for a naval force to reinforce Sumter would. The Confederate commissioners, who had been permitted to remain in Washington for an answer to their application to be accredited, were in some way secretly advised of every important measure of the Administration almost as soon as it was under consideration. These would have taken instant alarm had a statement of the naval force been bluntly called for by the President while the course in regard to Sumter was being discussed, or if made by the Secretary for naval purposes; but when asked for revenue purposes their apprehensions remained undisturbed. It was all-important for the new Administration to gain time, and the President with shrewdness and forbearance wisely kept his own counsel and asked for naval information for a necessary purpose which excited no alarm, and did not disturb the Secretary of State or General Scott, who advised forcible collection of the revenues. It was not until ten days later, and every day was precious, that he surprised his immediate advisers and friends as well as his opponents by announcing his intention to send supplies and reinforcements to Sumter. His purpose and determination he had wisely kept to himself; and in referring the letter of Major Anderson to General Scott, to ascertain the military view of the subject, as well as in subsequent Cabinet consultations to obtain the opinions of his associates, he was reserved; but he never, at any time, wavered from the principles and stand taken at the beginning of his administration, and enunciated in his inaugural address. His Cabinet and others concluded, from his reference of the subject to the General-in-Chief, that the reinforcement of Sumter was to be disposed of as a military question, and consequently acquiesced in the report of Generals Scott and Totten, but the President himself did not deviate from his original design. A knowledge of the military and naval resources at his disposal was, however, necessary, and without imparting his intention, and to cover his purpose, he inquired what force could be "at once placed at the control of the revenue service." Neither the Secretary of State nor General Scott supposed that this information was sought for any other than revenue purposes. Sumter they supposed was, as they had recommended, to be abandoned, and they beyond all others were overwhelmed with surprise when ten days later, the President announced his determination, so contrary to their advice and expectations. The sagacity, decision, and administrative and executive ability of Mr. Lincoln are exemplified in the skilful manner by which he lulled the suspicions of such of his immediate counsellors as favored a different policy in regard to Fort Sumter. It was the first exhibition of his independent self-reliance, and was conclusive that while he counselled with others, he was himself the President, and acted upon his own convictions.

3

Administration of Abraham Lincoln, I

Because of Lincoln's selection of a cabinet consisting
of representatives of rival factions, it was difficult to
maintain harmony among his advisers. In this essay,
Welles continues his account of the early months of
Lincoln's administration. Seward's attempts to interfere
with the plans for the relief of Fort Sumter, the difficulties confronting the Cabinet because of General
McClellan's imperious manners, the beginnings of the
split between radical and conservative Republicans constitute the high points of this article.

THE POLITICAL DIFFERENCES which have generated
parties in this country date back to an early period. They existed
under the old confederation, were perceptible in the formation
of the Constitution and establishment of "a more perfect union."
Differences on fundamental principles of government led to the
organization of parties which, under various names, after the
adoption of the Federal Constitution, divided the people and
influenced and often controlled national and State elections.
Neither of the parties, however, has always strictly adhered or
been true to its professed principles. Each has, under the pressure of circumstances and to secure temporary ascendancy in the
Federal or State governments, departed from the landmarks
and traditions which gave it its distinctive character. The *Centralists,* a name which more significantly than any other
expresses the character, principles, and tendency of those who
favor centralization of power in a supreme head that shall ex-

The Galaxy, XXIII (January, 1877).

ercise paternal control over States and people, have under various names constituted one party. On the other hand, the *Statists,* under different names, have from the first been jealous of central supremacy. They believe in local self-government, support the States in all their reserved and ungranted rights, insist on a strict construction of the Constitution and the limitation of Federal authority to the powers specifically delegated in that instrument.

The broad and deep line of demarcation between these parties has not always been acknowledged. Innovation and change have sometimes modified and disturbed this line; but after a period the distinctive boundary has reappeared and antagonized the people. During the administration of Mr. Monroe, known as the "era of good feeling," national party lines were almost totally obliterated, and local and personal controversies took their place. National questions were revived, however, and contested with extreme violence during several succeeding administrations. Thirty years later, when the issues of bank, tariff, internal improvements, and an independent treasury were disposed of, there was as complete a break-up of parties as in the days of Monroe. It was not, however, in an "era of good feeling" that this later dislocation of parties took place; but an attempt was made in 1850 by leading politicians belonging to different organizations to unite the people by a compromise or an arrangement as unnatural as it was insincere—party lines if not obliterated were, as the authors intended, in a measure broken down. This compromise, as it was called, was a sacrifice of honest principles, and instead of allaying disputes, was followed by a terrific storm of contention and violence transcending anything the country had ever experienced, and ended in a civil war.

The time has not yet arrived for a calm and dispassionate review of the acts and actors of that period and the events of the immediately succeeding years; but the incidents that took place and the experience so dearly purchased should not be perverted, misunderstood, or wholly forgotten.

The compromise of 1850, instead of adjusting differences and making the people of one mind on political questions, actu-

ally caused in their practical results the alienation of life-long
party friends, led to new associations among old opponents, and
created organizations that partook more of a sectional character
than of honest constitutional differences on fundamental questions relative to the powers and authority of the Government,
such as had previously divided the people. The facility with
which old political opponents came together in the compromise
measures of 1850, and abandoned principles and doctrines for
which they had battled through their whole lives, begot popular
distrust. Confidence in the sincerity of the men who so readily
made sacrifices of principles was forfeited or greatly impaired.
The Whig party dwindled under it, and as an organization
shortly went out of existence. A large portion of its members,
disgusted with what they considered the insincerity if not faith-
lessness of their leaders, yet unwilling to attach themselves to the
Democratic party, which had coalesced in the movement, gathered together in a secret organization, styling themselves "Know
Nothings." Democrats in some quarters, scarcely less dissatisfied
with the compromises, joined the Know Nothing order, and in
one or two annual elections this strange combination, without
avowed principles or purpose, save that of the defeat and overthrow of politicians, who were once their trusted favorites, was
successful. In this demoralized condition of affairs, the Democrats by the accession of Whigs in the Southern States obtained
possession of the Government and maintained their ascendancy
through the Pierce administration; and, in a contest quite as
much sectional as political, elected Buchanan in 1856.

But these were the expiring days of the old Democratic organization, which, under the amalgamating process of the
compromise measures, became shattered and mixed, especially
in the Southern States with former Whigs, and was to a great
extent thereafter sectionalized. The different opposing political
elements united against it and organized and established the Republican party, which triumphed in the election of Lincoln in
1860. The administration which followed and was inaugurated
in 1861 differed in essential particulars from either of the preceding political organizations. Men of opposing principles—
Centralists, who like Hamilton and patriots of that class were

for a strong imperial national government, with supervising and controlling authority over the States, on one hand, and Statists on the other, who, like Jefferson, adhered to State individuality and favored a league or federation of States, a national republic of limited and clearly defined powers, with a strict observance of all the reserved right of the local commonwealths—were brought together in the elections of 1860. It has been represented and recorded as grave history that the Republican party was an abolition party. Such was not the fact, although the small and utterly powerless faction which, under the lead of William Lloyd Garrison and others, had for years made aggressive war on slavery, was one of the elements which united with Whigs and Democrats in the election of Mr. Lincoln. Nor was that result a Whig triumph, though a large portion of the Whigs in the free States, after the compromises of 1850, from natural antagonism to the Democrats, entered into the Republican organization. While it is true that a large majority of the Whigs of the North relinquished their old organization and became Republicans, it is no less true that throughout the slave States, and in many of the free States, the members of the Whig party to a considerable extent supported Bell or Breckenridge. But Democrats dissatisfied with the measures of the Pierce and Buchanan administrations, in much larger numbers than is generally conceded, took early and efficient part in the Republican organizations—some on account of the repeal of the Missouri compromise, but a much larger number in consequence of the efforts of the central Government at Washington, by what was considered by them an abuse of civil trust, and by military interference, to overpower the settlers in Kansas, denying them the right of self-government, and an attempt arbitrarily and surreptitiously to impose upon the inhabitants against their will a fraudulent Constitution. It was this large contribution of free-thinking and independent Democrats, who had the courage to throw off party allegiance and discipline in behalf of the principles of free government on which our republican system is founded, the right of the people to self-government, and, consequently, the right to form and establish their own constitution without dictation or inter-

ference from the central government so long as they violated
no provision of the organic law, that gave tone, form, and
ascendancy to the Republican party in every free State.

Persistent efforts have been made to establish as historical
truths the representations that the civil war had its origin in a
scheme or purpose to abolish slavery in the States where it
existed, and that the election of Abraham Lincoln was an abolition triumph—a premeditated, aggressive, sectional war upon
the South; whereas the reverse is the fact—the Republican party
in its inception was a strictly constitutional party, that defended
the rights of the people, the rights of the States, and the rights of
the Federal Government, which were assailed by a sectional combination that was not satisfied with the Constitution as it was,
but proposed to exact new guarantees from the nation for the
protection of what they called "Southern rights"—rights unknown to the Constitution. The misrepresentations that the
Republicans were aggressive and aimed to change the organic
law have not been without their influence, temporarily at least,
in prejudicing and warping the public mind. It is true that the
slavery question was most injudiciously and unwisely brought
into the party controversies of the country; but it was done by
the slaveholders or their political representatives in Congress
after the failure of the nullifiers to obtain ascendancy in the
Government on the subject of free trade and resistance to the
revenue laws.

John C. Calhoun, a man of undoubted talents, but of unappeasable ambition, had at an early period of his life, while
Secretary of War, and still a young man, aspired to the office of
President. By his ability and patriotic course during the war of
1812, and subsequently by a brilliant career as a member of Mr.
Monroe's Cabinet, he had acquired fame and a certain degree
of popularity which favored his pretensions, particularly with
young men and army officers. Schemes and projects of national
aggrandizement by internal improvements, protection to home
industries, large military expenditures, and measures of a centralized tendency which were popular in that era of no parties,
gave him *éclat* as Secretary of War. Flattered by his attentions
and by his shining qualities, military men became his enthusi-

astic supporters, and received encouragement from him in return. It was the first attempt to elect so young a man to be
Chief Magistrate, and was more personal than political in its
character. In the memorable contest for the successorship to
President Monroe, Mr. Calhoun at one time seemed to be a
formidable candidate; but his popularity being personal was
evanescent, and failed to enlist the considerate and reflecting.
Even his military hopes were soon eclipsed by General Jackson,
whose bold achievements and successes in the Indian and British
wars captivated the popular mind. Jackson had also, as a representative and Senator in Congress, Judge of the Supreme Court
of Tennessee, and Governor of Florida, great civil experience.
Mr. Calhoun was, however, in the political struggle that took
place in 1824, elected to the second office of the republic, while
in the strife, confusion, and break-up of parties no one of the
competing candidates for President received a majority of the
electoral votes. He and his supporters submitted to, it may be
said acquiesced in, the result then and also in 1828, when
General Jackson was elected President and Mr. Calhoun was
reëlected to the office of Vice-President. This acquiescence,
however, was reluctant; but with an expectation that he would
in 1833, at the close of General Jackson's term, be the successor
of the distinguished military chieftain.

But the arrangements of calculating politicians often end in
disappointments. Such was the misfortune of Mr. Calhoun.
His ambitious and apparently well contrived plans had most
of them an abortive and hapless termination. Observation and
experience convinced him, after leaving Mr. Monroe's Cabinet,
that the educated and reflective Statists or State rights men of
the country, and especially of the South, would never sanction
or be reconciled to the exercise of power by the Federal Government to protect the manufacturing interests of New England, or
to construct roads and canals in the West, at the expense of the
National Treasury. These were, however, favorite measures of a
class of politicians of the period who had special interests to
subserve, and who carried with them the consolidationists, or
advocates of a strong and magnificent central government. The
tariff, internal improvements, and kindred subjects became

classified and known in the party politics of that day as the "American system"—a system of high taxes and large expenditures by the Federal Government—without specific constitutional authority for either. Parties were arrayed on opposite sides of this system, which, besides the political principles involved, soon partook of a sectional character. High and oppressive duties on importations, it was claimed, were imposed to foster industries in the North to the injury of the South.

Henry Clay, a politician and statesman of wonderful magnetic power, was the eloquent champion of the "American system," and enlisted in his favor the large manufacturing interest in the North and the friends of internal improvement in the West. These measures were made national issues, and Mr. Clay, Speaker of the House of Representatives, appropriated them to his personal advancement, and was their recognized leading advocate. Mr. Calhoun could not be second to his Western rival, but abandoned the policy of protection, internal improvements, and great national undertakings, and allied himself to the commercial and plantation interests, which opposed the system, expecting to identify himself with and to receive the support of the Statists. But the strict constructionists of Virginia, Georgia, and other states of the old Jefferson school distrusted him and withheld their confidence and support.

South Carolina, erratic, brilliant, and impulsive, had never fully harmonized with the politicians of Virginia in their political doctrines, but had been inclined to ridicule the rigid and non-progressive principles of her statesmen, who, always cautious, were now slow to receive into fellowship and to commit themselves to the new convert who sought their support. They slighted him, and rejected his nullification remedies. Instead of following the Palmetto State in her fanatical party schemes on the alleged issue of free trade, and supporting her "favorite son" in his theories, they sustained General Jackson, whose Union sentiments they approved, and who, to the disgust of Calhoun, became a candidate for reëlection in 1832 and received the votes of almost the whole South.

In this crisis, when the heated partisans of South Carolina in their zeal for free trade and State rights had made a step

in advance of the more staid and reflecting Statists, and undertook to abrogate and nullify the laws of the Federal Government legally enacted, they found themselves unsupported and
in difficulty, and naturally turned to their acknowledged leader
for guidance. To contest the Federal Government, and pioneer
the way for his associates to resist and overthrow the Administration, Mr. Calhoun resigned the office of Vice-President and
accepted that of Senator, where his active mind, fertile in resources, could, and as he and they believed would extricate
them. There was, however, at the head of the Government in
that day a stern, patriotic, and uncompromising Chief Magistrate, who would listen to no mere temporizing expedients
when the stability of the Union was involved, and who, while
recognizing and maintaining the rights of the States, never for-
got the rights that belonged to the Federal Government. In his
extremity, when confronting this inflexible President, Mr.
Calhoun hastened to make friends with his old opponents, Clay,
Webster, and the protectionists, the advocates of the "American
system," the authors and champions of the very policy which
had been made the pretext or justification for nullification and
resistance to Federal law and the Federal authority. This coalition of hostile factions combined in a scheme, or compromise,
where each sacrificed principles to oppose the administration of
Jackson. It was an insincere and unrighteous coalition which
soon fell asunder.

In the mean time, while nullification was hopelessly pros-
trate, and before the coalition was complete, the prolific mind
of the aspiring Carolinian devised a new plan and a new system of tactics which it was expected would sectionalize and
unite the South. This new device was a defence of slavery—a
subject in which the entire South was interested—against the
impudent demands of the abolitionists. Not until the nullifiers
were defeated, and had failed to draw the South into their
nullification plan, was slavery agitation introduced into Congress and made a sectional party question with aggressive demands for national protection. The abolitionists were few
in numbers, and of little account in American politics. Some
benevolent Quakers and uneasy fanatics, who neither compre-

hended the structure of our Federal system nor cared for the
Constitution, had annually for forty years petitioned Congress to
give freedom to the slaves. But the statesmen of neither party
listened to these unconstitutional appeals until the defeated
nullifiers professed great apprehension in regard to them, and
introduced the subject as a disturbance, and made it a sensa-
tional sectional issue in Congress and the elections.

From the first agitation of the subject as a party question,
slavery in all its phases was made sectional and aggressive by
the South. Beginning with a denial of the right to petition for
the abolition of slavery, and with demands for new and more
exacting national laws for the arrest and rendition of fugitives,
the new sectional party test was followed by other measures;
such as the unconditional admission of Texas, the extension of
slavery into all the free territory acquired from Mexico, the
repeal of the Missouri compromise, a denial to the people of
Kansas of the right to frame their own constitution, and other
incidental and irritating questions that were not legitimately
within the scope of Federal authority. Fierce contentions prevailed for years, sometimes more violent than at others.

In 1850 a budget of compromises, which has already been
alluded to, involving a surrender of principles and an enactment
of laws that were unwarranted by the Constitution, and offensive in other respects, had been patched up by old Congressional
party leaders, ostensibly to reconcile conflicting views and interests, but which were superficial remedies for a cancerous disease,
and intended more to glorify the authors than to promote the
country's welfare. Both of the great parties were committed by
the managers to these compromises, but the effect upon each
was different. The Whigs, tired of constant defeat, hoped for a
change by the compromises that would give them recognition
and power; but instead of these they found themselves dwarfed
and weakened, while the Democrats, who yielded sound principles to conciliate their Southern allies, were for a time numeri-
cally strengthened in that section by accessions from the Whigs.
Old party lines became broken, and in the Presidential contest
of 1852 the Democratic candidate, General Pierce, a young and
showy, but not profound man, was elected by an overwhelming

majority over the veteran General Scott, who was the candidate
of the Whigs. From this date the Whig organization dwindled
and had but a fragmentary existence. Thenceforward, until the
overthrow of the Democratic party, the Government at Washington tended to centralization. Fidelity to party, and adherence
to organization, with little regard for principle, were its political tests in the free States. Sectional sentiments to sustain
Southern aggressions, under the name of "Southern rights," were
inculcated, violent language, and acts that were scarcely less
so, prevailed through the South and found apologists and
defenders at the North. Presidents Pierce and Buchanan, literally "northern men with southern principles," were submissive
to these sectional aggressions, acquiesced in the repeal of the
Missouri compromise, the extension and nationalizing of slavery, hitherto a State institution, and also to the schemes to
prevent the establishment of a free constitution by the people
of Kansas. The mass of voters opposed to the policy of these administrations, and who constituted the Republican party, were
not entirely in accord on fundamental principles and views of
government, but had been brought into united action from the
course of events which followed the Mexican war, the acquisition
of territory, and the unfortunate compromises of 1850. The sectional strife, for the alleged reason of Lincoln's election and Republican success, which eventuated in hostilities in 1861, and the
tremendous conflict that succeeded and shook the foundation of
the Government during the ensuing four years, threatening the
national existence, absorbed all minor questions of a purely
political party character, and made the Cabinet of Mr. Lincoln, though its members entertained organic differences, a
unit. There were occasions when the antecedent opinions and
convictions of the members elicited discussion in regard to the
powers, limitations, and attributes of government; but in the
midst of war disagreeing political opinions as well as the laws
themselves were silenced. Each and all felt the necessity of harmonious and efficient action to preserve the Union.

This was especially the case during the first two years of
the war of secession. Not only the President's constitutional
advisers, but the Republican members of Congress, embracing

many captious, factious, and theoretical controversialists, acted in harmony and concert. Murmurs were heard among its friends, and dissatisfaction felt that the Administration was not sufficiently energetic or arbitrary, and because it did not immediately suppress the rebellion. A long period of peace which the country had enjoyed rendered the malcontents incapable of judging of the necessities of preparation for war. "On to Richmond" became the cry of the impatient and restless before the armies mustered into service were organized. The violent and impassioned appeals of excited and mischievous speakers and writers created discontent and clamor that could not always be appeased or successfully resisted. Not content with honest if not always intelligent criticism of the Government, some editors, papers, writers, and speakers, at an early period and indeed throughout the war, condemned the policy pursued, assumed to direct the management of affairs, and advanced crude and absurd notions of the manner in which the Government should be administered and military operations conducted. For a period after the rout at Bull Run, which seemed a rebuke to these inconsiderate partisans, there was a temporary lull of complaints and apparent acquiescence by Republicans in the measures of administration.

Military differences and army jealousies existed from the beginning, which were aggravated and stimulated by partisan friends and opponents of the rival officers, and by dissent from the policy pursued in the conduct of military affairs to which many took exception.

General Scott was the military oracle of the Administration in the first days of the war. His ability and great experience entitled him to regard and deference on all questions relating to military operations. No one appreciated his qualities more than the President, unless it was General Scott himself, who with great self-esteem was nevertheless not unconscious that his age and infirmities had impaired his physical energies, and in some respects unfitted him to be the active military commander. It was his misfortune that he prided himself more if possible on his civil and political knowledge and his administrative ability than on his military skill and capacity. As a poli-

tician his opinions were often chimerical, unstable, and of little
moment; but his military knowledge and experience were
valuable. With headquarters at Washington, and for thirty
years consulted and trusted by successive administrations of
different parties in important emergencies, internal and external, and at one time the selected candidate of one of the
great political parties for President, he had reason to feel that
he was an important personage in the republic; also that he
was competent, and that it was a duty for him to participate
in political matters, and to advise in civil affairs when there
were threatened dangers. But while he was sagacious to detect
the premonitory symptoms of disturbance, and always ready to
obey and execute military orders, he was in political and civil
matters often weak, irresolute, and infirm of purpose. He had
in the autumn of 1860 warned President Buchanan of danger
to be apprehended from the secession movement, and wisely
suggested measures to preserve peace; but he soon distrusted
and abandoned his own suggestions. Without much knowledge
of Mr. Lincoln, and believing erroneously, as did many others,
that Mr. Seward was to be the controlling mind in the new administration, he early put himself in communication with that
gentleman. The two agreed upon the policy of surrendering
or yielding to the States in secession the fortresses within their
respective limits. It has been said, and circumstances indicate
that there was also an understanding by Mr. Seward with
certain secession leaders, that the forts, particularly Sumter, if
not attacked, should not be reinforced. Of the plans of Mr.
Seward and General Scott, and the understanding which either
of them had with the secessionists, President Lincoln was not
informed; but, while he had a sense of duty and policy of his
own, he attentively and quietly listened to each and to all
others entitled to give their opinions.

The reports of Major Anderson and the defence of Sumter
being military operations, the President, pursuant to Mr.
Seward's advice, referred to General Scott, and it was supposed
by those gentlemen that the President acquiesced in their conclusions. Nor were they alone in that supposition, for the
President, while cautiously feeling his way, sounding the minds

of others, and gathering information from every quarter, wisely
kept his own counsel and delayed announcing his determination
until the last moment. He was accused to being culpably slow,
when he was wisely deliberate.

When his decision to reinforce Sumter was finally made
known, the Secretary of State and the General-in-Chief were
surprised, embarrassed, and greatly disappointed; for it was an
utter negation and defeat of the policy which they had prescribed. The General, like a good soldier, quietly and submis-
sively acquiesced; but Mr. Seward, a man of expedients and
some conceit, was unwilling and unprepared to surrender the
first place in the Administration, and virtually publish the
fact by an Executive mandate which upset his promised and
preferred arrangements. It was then that he became aware
of two things: first, that neither himself nor General Scott, nor
both combined, were infallible with the Administration, and
second, that the President, with all his suavity and genial nature,
had a mind of his own, and the resolution and self-reliance to
form, and the firmness and independence to execute a purpose.
They had each overestimated the influence of the other with
the President, and underestimated his capacity, will, and self-
reliance. When the Secretary became convinced that he could
not alter the President's determination, he conformed to circumstances, immediately changed his tactics, and after notifying
the authorities at Charleston that the garrison in Sumter was
to be supplied, he took prompt but secret measures to defeat the
expedition by detaching the flagship, and sending her, with the
supplies and reinforcements that had been prepared and intended for Sumter, to Fort Pickens. In doing this he consulted
neither the War nor Navy Departments, to which the service
belonged; but discarding both, and also the General-in-Chief,
his preceding special confidant, and with whom he had until
then acted in concert, he took to his counsel younger military
officers, secretly advised with them and withdrew them from
their legitimate and assigned duties. The discourtesy and the
irregularity of the proceeding, when it became known, shocked
General Scott. His pride was touched. He felt the slight, but he
was too good an officer, too subordinate, and too well disciplined,

to complain. The secret military expedition undertaken by the
Secretary of State without the knowledge of the proper departments and of himself, was so irregular, such evidence of improper administration, that he became alarmed. He felt keenly
the course of Mr. Seward in not consulting him, and in substituting one of his staff as military adviser for the Secretary of
State; but he was more concerned for the Government and
country.

A native of Virginia, and imbued with the political doctrines
there prevalent, but unflinching in patriotism and devotion to
the Union and the flag, General Scott hesitated how to act—
objected to the hostile invasion of any State by the national
troops, but advised that the rebellious section should be
blockaded by sea and land. He thought that surrounded by the
army and navy the insurgents would be cut off from the outer
world, and when exhausted from non-intercourse and the entire
prostration of trade and commerce they would return to duty;
the "anaconda principle" of exhausting them he believed would
be effectual without invading the territory of States. When the
mayor of Baltimore and a committee of secessionists waited upon
the President on the 20th of April to protest against the passage
of troops through that city to the national capital, he, in deference to the local government, advised the President to yield to
the metropolitan demand, and himself drew up an Executive
order to that effect. The seizure of Harper's Ferry and Norfolk
and the threatened attack upon Washington greatly disturbed
him, but not so much as the wild cry of the ardent and impulsive
which soon followed of "on to Richmond" with an undisciplined
army.

Sensible of his inability to take the field, he acquiesced in
the selection if he did not propose after the disaster at Bull
Run, that General McClellan should be called to Washington
to organize the broken and demoralized Army of the Potomac.
A thorough reorganization was promptly and effectually accomplished by that officer. In a few days order, precision, and
discipline prevailed—the troops were massed and a large army
was encamped in and about the national capital. But it was soon
evident to the members of the Administration that there was

not perfect accord between the two Generals. The cause and extent of disagreement were not immediately understood.

At a Cabinet meeting which took place in September at the headquarters of the General-in-Chief by reason of his physical infirmities, a brief discussion occurred which developed coolness if not dissatisfaction. An inquiry was made by the President as to the exact number of troops then in and about Washington. General McClellan did not immediately respond—said he had brought no reports or papers with him. General Scott said he had not himself recently received any reports. Secretary Seward took from his pocket some memoranda, stating the number that had been mustered in a few days previous, and then went on to mention additional regiments which had arrived several successive days since, making an aggregate, I think, of about ninety-three thousand men. The General immediately became grave.

When the subject matter for which the Cabinet and war officers had been convened was disposed of, some of the gentlemen left, and General McClellan was about retiring, when General Scott requested him to remain, and he also desired the President and the rest of us to listen to some inquiries and remarks which he wished to make. He was very deliberate, but evidently very much aggrieved. Addressing General McClellan, he said:

"You are perhaps aware, General McClellan, that you were brought to these headquarters by my advice and by my orders after consulting with the President. I know you to be intelligent and to be possessed of some excellent military qualities; and after our late disaster it appeared to me that you were a proper person to organize and take active command of this army. I brought you here for that purpose. Many things have been, as I expected they would be, well done; but in some respects I have been disappointed. You do not seem to be aware of your true position; and it was for this reason I desired that the President and these gentlemen should hear what I have to say. You are here upon my staff to obey my orders, and should daily report to me. This you have failed to do, and you appear to labor under the mistake of supposing that you and not I are General-in-Chief and in command of the armies. I more than you am responsible for military operations; but since you came here I have been in no condition to give directions or to advise the President because my chief of staff has neglected to make reports to me. I cannot answer simple inquiries which the President or any member of the Cabinet makes as to the number of troops here; they must go to the State department and not come to military headquarters for that information."

Mr. Seward here interposed to say that the statement he had made was from facts which he had himself collected from day to day as the troops arrived. "Do I understand," asked General Scott, "that the regiments report as they come here to the Honorable Secretary of State?"

"No, no," said Mr. Cameron, who wished to arrest or soften a painful interview. "General McClellan is not to blame; it is Seward's work. He is constantly meddling with what is none of his business, and (alluding to the Pickens expedition) makes mischief in the war and navy departments by his interference."

There was in the manner more than in the words a playful sarcasm which Seward felt and the President evidently enjoyed. General McClellan stood by the open door with one hand raised and holding it, a good deal embarrassed. He said he had intended no discourtesy to General Scott, but he had been so incessantly occupied in organizing and placing the army, receiving and mustering in the recruits as they arrived, and attending to what was absolutely indispensable, that it might seem he omitted some matters of duty, but he should extremely regret if it was supposed he had been guilty of any disrespect.

"You are too intelligent and too good a disciplinarian not to know your duties and the proprieties of military intercourse," said General Scott; "but seem to have misapprehended your right position. I, you must understand, am General-in-Chief. You are my chief of staff. When I brought you here you had my confidence and friendship. I do not say that you have yet entirely lost my confidence. Good day, General McClellan."

A few weeks later General Scott was on his own application placed upon the retired list, and General McClellan became his successor. Disaffection on the part of any of the officers, if any existed, did not immediately show itself; the army and

people witnessed with pride the prompt and wonderful reorganization that had taken place, and for a time exulted in the
promised efficiency and capabilities of the "young Napoleon."
But the autumn passed away in grand reviews and showy parades, where the young General appeared with a numerous staff
composed of wealthy young gentlemen, inexperienced, untrained,
and unacquainted with military duty, who as well as foreign
princes had volunteered their services. Parades and reviews
were not useless, and the committal of wealthy and influential
citizens who were placed up his staff had its advantages; but
as time wore on and no blow was struck or any decisive movement attempted, complaints became numerous and envy and
jealousy found opportunity to be heard.

The expectation that the rebellion would be suppressed in
ninety days, and that an undisciplined force of seventy-five
thousand men or even five times that number would march to
Richmond, clear the banks of the Mississippi, capture New
Orleans, and overwhelm the whole South, had given way to
more reasonable and rational views before Congress convened
at the regular session in December. Still the slow progress that
was made by the Union armies, and the immense war expenditures, to which our country was then unaccustomed, caused uneasiness with the people, and furnished food and excitement
for the factions in Congress.

The anti-slavery feeling was increasing, but efforts to effect
emancipation were not controlling sentiments of the Administration or of a majority of Congress at the commencement or
during the first year of Mr. Lincoln's term, although such are
the representations of party writers, and to some extent of the
historians of the period. Nor did the Administration, as is often
asserted and by many believed, commence hostilities and make
aggressive war on the slave States or their institutions; but when
war began and a national garrison in a national fortress was
attacked, it did not fail to put forth its power and energies
to suppress the rebellion and maintain the integrity of the
Union. Military delays and tardy movements were nevertheless
charged to the imbecility of the Government. It is not to be
denied that a portion of the most active supporters of the Pres-

ident in and out of Congress and in the armies had in view
ulterior purposes than that of suppressing the insurrection. Some
were determined to avail themselves of the opportunity to
abolish slavery, others to extinguish the claim of reserved
sovereignty to the States, and a portion were favorable to both
of these extremes and to the consolidation of power in the central Government; but a larger number than either and perhaps
more than all combined were for maintaining the Constitution
and Union unimpaired.

The President, while opposed to all innovating schemes, had
the happy faculty of so far harmonizing and reconciling his
differing friends as to keep them united in resisting the secession
movement.

Abraham Lincoln was in many respects a remarkable man,
never while living fully understood or appreciated. An uncultured child of the frontiers, with no educational advantages,
isolated in youth in his wilderness home, with few associates and
without family traditions, he knew not his own lineage and
connections. Nor was this singular in the then condition of unsettled frontier life. His grandfather, with Daniel Boone, left
the settled part of Virginia, crossed the Alleghany mountains,
penetrated the "dark and bloody ground," and took up his
residence in the wilds of Kentucky near the close of the Revolutionary war. There was little intercourse with each other in
the new and scattered settlements destitute of roads and with no
mail facilities for communication with relatives, friends, and
the civilized world east of the mountains. Abraham Lincoln,
the grandfather of the President, was a nephew of Daniel Boone,
and partook of the spirit of his brave and subsequently famous
relative. But his residence in his secluded home was brief. He
was killed by the Indians when his son Thomas, the father of
President Lincoln, was only six years. Four years later the
fatherless boy lost his mother. Left an orphan, this neglected
child, without kith or kindred for whom he cared or who cared
for him, led a careless, thriftless life, became a wandering
pioneer, emigrated from Kentucky when the President was but
seven years old, took up his residence for several years in the
remote solitudes of Indiana, and drifted at a later day to Illi-

nois. This vagrant life, by a shiftless father, and without a
mother or female relative to keep alive and impress upon him
the pedigree and traditions of his family, left the President
without definite knowledge of his origin and that of his fathers.
The deprivation he keenly felt. I heard him say on more than
one occasion that when he laid down his official life he would
endeavor to trace out his genealogy and family history. He had
a vague impression that his family had emigrated from England
to Pennsylvania and thence to Virginia; but, as he remarked in
my presence to Mr. Ashmun of Massachusetts, and afterward to
Governor Andrew, there was not, he thought, any immediate
connection with the families of the same name in Massachusetts,
though there was reason to suppose they had a common ancestry.

Having entered upon this subject, and already said more than
was anticipated at the commencement, the opportunity is fitting
to introduce extracts from a statement made by himself and
to accompany it with other facts which have come into my possession since his death—facts of which he had no knowledge.

In a brief autobiographical sketch of his life, written by
himself, he says:

I was born February 12, 1809, in Hardin county, Kentucky. My parents were both born in Virginia, of undis-
tinguished families—second families perhaps I should say.
My mother, who died in my tenth year, was of a family
of the name of Hanks, some of whom now reside in Adams
and others in Macon county, Illinois. My paternal grandfather, Abraham Lincoln, emigrated from Rockingham
county, Virginia, to Kentucky, about 1781 or 2, where, a
year or two later, he was killed by Indians, not in battle,
but by stealth, when he was laboring to open a farm in the
forest. His ancestors, who were Quakers, went to Virginia
from Berks county, Pennsylvania. An effort to identify them
with the New England family of the same name ended in
nothing more definite than a similarity of Christian names
in both families, such as Enoch, Levi, Mordecai, Solomon,
Abraham, and the like.

My father, at the death of his father, was but six years
of age; and he grew up literally without education. He removed from Kentucky to what is now Spencer county,

Indiana, in my eighth year. We reached our new home about the time the State came into the Union. It was a wild region, with many bears and other wild animals still in the woods. There I grew up. There were some schools, so called; but no qualification was ever required of a teacher, beyond reading, writing, and ciphering to the rule of three. If a straggler, supposed to understand Latin, happened to sojourn in the neighborhood, he was looked upon as a wizard. There was absolutely nothing to excite ambition for education. Of course when I came of age I did not know much. Still, somehow, I could read, write, and cipher, to the rule of three; but that was all. I have not been to schools since. The little advance I now have upon this store of education I have picked up from time to time under the pressure of necessity.

I was raised to farm work, which I continued till I was twenty-two. At twenty-two I came to Illinois, and passed the first year in Macon county. Then I got to New Salem, at that time in Sangamon, now in Menard county, where I remained a year as a sort of clerk in a store.

In addition to the foregoing I may add that among my acquaintance in central Pennsylvania were several sisters whose maiden name was Winters. Two of these sisters were wives of Judges of the Supreme Court of Pennsylvania. Another sister was the wife of William Potter, a member of Congress of some note from that State and son of General Potter of the Revolution. These sisters were the great aunts of President Lincoln, and I subjoin an obituary notice of the younger sister, Mrs. Potter, who died in 1875, at the advanced age of eighty-four. There are some incidents not immediately connected with the subject that might be omitted, but I think it best to present the obituary in full:

Died in Bellefonte, at the residence of Edward C. Humes, on Sunday morning, the 30th of May A.D. 1875, Mrs. Lucy Potter, relict of Hon. William W. Potter, deceased, aged eighty-four years, nine months, and two days.

Mrs. Potter was a member of a large and rather remarkable family; her father having been born in 1728, married in 1747, died in 1794; children to the number of nineteen be-

ing born to him, the eldest in 1748, the youngest in 1790—
their birth extending over a period of forty-two years. William Winters, the father of the deceased, came from Berks
county to Northumberland, now Lycoming county, in the
year 1778, having purchased the farm lately known as the
Judge Grier farm, near what was called Newberry, but now
within the corporate limits of the city of Williamsport. Mr.
Winters was twice married. His first wife was Ann Boone, a
sister of Colonel Daniel Boone, famous in the early annals of
Kentucky. His marriage took place in the year 1747 in the
then province of Virginia. By this union there were issue
eleven children, four males and seven females. His eldest
daughter, Hannah, married in Rockingham county, Virginia, Abraham Lincoln, the grandfather of President Lincoln. Shortly before his death, Lincoln, who was killed by
the Indians, visited his father-in-law at what is now Williamsport, and John Winters, his brother-in-law, returned
with him to Kentucky, whither Mr. Lincoln had removed
after his marriage; John being deputed to look after some
lands taken by Colonel Daniel Boone and his father.

They traveled on foot from the farm, by a route leading
by where Bellefonte now is, the Indian path "leading from
Bald Eagle to Frankstown."

John Winters visited his sister, Mrs. Potter, in 1843, and
wandering to the hill upon which the Academy is situated,
a messenger was sent for him, his friends thinking he had
lost himself; but he was only looking for the path he and
Lincoln had trod sixty years before, and pointed out with
his finger the course from Spring creek, along Buffalo
run, to where it crosses the "Long Limestone Valley," as
the route they had travelled.

Upon the death of Mr. Winter's first wife, in 1771, he
again, in 1774, married. His second wife was Ellen Camp-
bell, who bore him eight children, three males and five
females, of which latter the subject of this notice was the
youngest.

The father of Mrs. Potter died in 1794, and in 1795
Mrs. Ellen Winters, his widow, was licensed by the courts
of Lycoming county to keep a "house of entertainment"
where Williamsport now is—where she lived and reared her
own children as well as several of her step children.

Here all her daughters married, Mary becoming the wife
of Charles Huston, who for a number of years adorned the
bench of the Supreme Court of this State; Ellen, the wife
of Thomas Burnside, who was a member of Congress, Judge
of the Court of Common Pleas, and finally a Justice of the
Supreme Court; Sarah, the wife of Benjamin Harris, whose
daughter, Miss Ellen Harris, resides on Spring street in this
borough; Elizabeth, the wife of Thomas Alexander, a car-
penter and builder, who erected one of the first dwellings
in Williamsport, at the corner of what are now Pine and
Third streets in that city, and many of whose descendants
are still living in Lycoming county; Lucy, the wife of William W. Potter, a leading politician in this county, who died
on the 15th day of October, 1838, while a member of our
national Congress.

Mrs. Potter continued with her mother's family in Lycoming county, frequently visiting her two sisters, Mrs.
Huston and Mrs. Burnside, who resided in Bellefonte,
where, in 1815, she was united in marriage, by Rev. James
Linn, with William W. Potter, a young and rising lawyer,
and son of General James Potter, one of the early settlers
of the county. Here, with her husband until his death,
and then, upon the marriage of her niece, Miss Lucy Alexander, with Mr. Edward C. Humes, she made her home,
living continuously in this town since her marriage, and
having survived her husband for the long period of thirty-
seven years, being that length of time a widow.

The biographers of President Lincoln have none of them
given these facts because they did not know them, nor was the
President himself aware of them. Of their authenticity so far
as the relationship of Mr. Lincoln with the family of Winters is
concerned, I have no doubt. His ancestry in this country, paternal and maternal—Lincoln, Boone, and Winters—is to be
traced to the county of Berks, Pennsylvania.

A roving child of the forest, where there were not even
village schools, Abraham Lincoln had little early culture, but
his vigorous native intellect sought information wherever it
could be obtained with limited means and opportunities and
overcame almost insuperable obstacles. His quick perception and

powers of observation and reflection, and his retentive memory were remarkable; his judgment was good, his mental grasp and comprehension equal to any emergency, his intentions were always honest, and his skill and tact, with a determination to always maintain the right, begot confidence and made him successful and great. Party opponents impute his success under difficulties that seemed insurmountable to craft and cunning; but while not deficient in shrewdness, his success was the result not of deceptive measures or wily intrigue, but of wisdom and fidelity with an intuitive sagacity that seldom erred as to measures to be adopted, or the course to be pursued. It may be said of him, that he possessed inherently a master mind, and was innately a leader of men. He listened, as I have often remarked, patiently to the advice and opinions of others, though he might differ from them; treated unintentional errors with lenity, was forbearing, and kind to mistaken subordinates, but ever true to his own convictions. He gathered information and knowledge whenever and wherever he had opportunity, but quietly put aside assumption and intrusive attempt to unduly influence and control him.

Like all his Cabinet, with the exception of Mr. Blair, who had been educated at West Point, he was without military pretension when he entered upon his executive duties and encountered at the very threshold a civil war which had been long maturing, was deeply seated, and in its progress was almost unprecedented in magnitude. Neither he nor any of his advisers had personal, official, practical experience in administering the civil service of the Federal Government. The commencement of hostilities, before they had time to become familiar with their duties, imposed upon each and all labors and cares beyond those of any of their predecessors. To these were added the conduct of military operations as novel as they were responsible. Unprepared as the country was for the sudden and formidable insurrection, the Administration was not less so, yet it was compelled at once to meet it, make preparations, call out immense armies, and select officers to organize and command them.

These commanders were most of them educated military officers, but possessed of limited experience. Their lives had

been passed on a peace establishment, and they were consequently without practical knowledge. Many of these, as well as such
officers as were selected from civil life, seemed bewildered by
their sudden preferment, and appeared to labor under the impression that they were clothed not only with military but civil
authority. Some in the higher grades imagined that in addition
to leading armies and fighting battles, they had plenary power
to administer the Government and prescribe the policy to be
pursued in their respective departments. Much difficulty and no
small embarrassment was caused by their mistaken assumptions
and acts, in the early part of the war.

J. C. Fremont, the western explorer, a political candidate for
the Presidency in 1856, and made a major general by President
Lincoln at the beginning of the rebellion in 1861, was assigned
to the command of the western department. He evidently
considered himself clothed with proconsular powers; that he
was a representative of the Government in a civil capacity as
well as military commander, and soon after establishing his
headquarters at St. Louis assumed authority over the slavery
question which the President could neither recognize nor permit. General Hunter, at Port Royal, and General Phelps, in the
Gulf, each laboring under the same error, took upon themselves
to issue extraordinary manifestoes that conflicted with the Constitution and laws, on the subject of slavery, which the President
was compelled to disavow. The subject, if to be acted upon, was
administrative and belonged to the Government and civil authorities—not to military commanders. But there was a feeling
in Congress and the country which sympathized with the radical
generals in these anti-slavery decrees, rather than with the law,
and the Executive in maintaining it. The Secretary of War,
under whom these generals acted, not inattentive to current
opinion, also took an extraordinary position, and in his annual
report enunciated a policy in regard to the slavery question,
without the assent of the President and without even consulting
him. Mr. Lincoln promptly directed the assuming portion of
the report, which had already been printed, to be cancelled; but
the proceeding embarrassed the Administration and contributed
to the retirement of Mr. Cameron from the Cabinet. These

differences in the army, in the Administration, and among the Republicans in Congress, extended to the people. A radical faction opposed to the legal, cautious, and considerate policy of the President began to crystallize and assume shape and form, which, while it did not openly oppose the President, sowed the seeds of discontent against his policy and the general management of public affairs.

The military operations of the period are not here detailed or alluded to, except incidentally when narrating the action of the Administration in directing army movements and shaping the policy of the Government. Nearly one-third of the States were, during the Presidency of Mr. Lincoln, unrepresented in the national councils, and in open rebellion. A belt of border States, extending from the Delaware to the Rocky mountains, which, though represented in Congress, had a divided population, was distrustful of the President. Yielding the Administration a qualified support, and opposed to the Government in almost all its measures, was an old organized and disciplined party in all the free States, which seemed to consider its obligations to party paramount to duty to the country. This last, if it did not boldly participate with the rebels, was an auxiliary, and as a party, hostile to the Administration, and opposed to nearly every measure for suppressing the insurrection.

There were among the friends of the Administration, and especially during its last two years, radical differences, which in the first stages of the war were undeveloped. The mild and persuasive temper of the President, his generous and tolerant disposition and his kind and moderate forbearance toward the rebels, whom he invited and would persuade to return to their allegiance and their duty, did not correspond with the schemes and designs of the extreme and violent leaders of the Republican party. They had other objects than reconstruction to attain, were implacable and revengeful, and some with ulterior radical views thought the opportunity favorable to effect a change of administration.

These had for years fomented division, encouraged strife, and were as ultra and as unreasonable in their demands and exactions as the secessionists. Some had welcomed war with

grim satisfaction, and were for prosecuting it unrelentingly
with fire and sword to the annihilation of the rights, and the
absolute subversion of the Southern States and subjection of the
Southern people. There was in their ranks unreasoning fanati-
cism, and ferocity that partook of barbarism, with a mixture
of political intrigue fatal to our Federal system. These men, dissatisfied with President Lincoln, accused him of temporizing,
of imbecility, and of sympathy with the rebels because he would
not confiscate their whole property, and hang or punish them
as pirates or traitors. These radical Republicans, as they were
proud to call themselves, occupied, like all extreme men in high
party and revolutionary times, the front rank of their party,
and, though really a minority, gave tone and character to the
Republican organization. Fired with avenging zeal, and often
successful in their extreme views, though to some extent
checked and modified by the President, they were presuming,
and flattered themselves they could, if unsuccessful with Mr.
Lincoln, effect a change in the administration of the Government
in 1864 by electing a President who would conform to their
ultra demands. Secret meetings and whispered consultations
were held for that purpose, and for a time aspiring and calculating politicians gave them encouragement; but it soon became
evident that the conservative sentiment of the Republicans
and the country was with Mr. Lincoln, and that the confidence
of the people in his patriotism and integrity was such as could
not be shaken. Nevertheless, a small band of the radicals held
out and would not assent to his benignant policy. These malcontents undertook to create a distinct political organization
which, if possessed of power, would make a more fierce and
unrelenting war on the rebels, break down their local institutions, overturn their State governments, subjugate the whites,
elevate the blacks, and give not only freedom to the slaves, but
by national decree override the States, and give suffrage to the
whole colored race. These extreme and rancorous notions found
no favor with Mr. Lincoln, who, though nominally a Whig in
the past, had respect for the Constitution, loved the Federal
Union, and had a sacred regard for the rights of the States,
which the Whigs as a party did not entertain. War two years

after secession commenced brought emancipation, but emancipation did not dissolve the Union, consolidate the Government, or clothe it with absolute power; nor did it impair the authority and rights which the States had reserved. Emancipation was a necessary, not a revolutionary measure, forced upon the Administration by the secessionists themselves, who insisted that slavery which was local and sectional should be made national.

The war was, in fact, defensive on the part of the Government against a sectional insurrection which had seized the fortresses and public property of the nation; a war for the maintainence of the Union, not for its dissolution; a war for the preservation of individual, State, and Federal rights; good administration would permit neither to be sacrificed nor one to encroach on the other. The necessary exercise of extraordinary war powers to suppress the Rebellion had given encouragement and strength to the centralists who advocated the consolidation and concentration of authority in the general Government in peace as well as war, and national supervision over the States and people. Neither the radical enthusiasts nor the designing centralists admitted or subscribed to the doctrine that political power emanated from the people; but it was the theory of both that the authority exercised by the States was by grant derived from the parental or general Government. It was their theory that the Government created the States, not that the States and people created the Government. Some of them had acquiesced in certain principles which were embodied in the fundamental law called the Constitution; but the Constitution was in their view the child of necessity, a mere crude attempt of the theorists of 1776, who made successful resistance against British authority, to limit the power of the new central Government which was substituted for that of the crown. For a period after the Revolution, it was admitted that feeble limitations on central authority had been observed, though it was maintained that those limitations had been obstructions to our advancing prosperity, the cause of continual controversy, and had gradually from time to time been dispensed with, broken down, or made to yield to our growing necessities. The civil war had made innovations—a sweep, in fact, of many constitutional barriers—and radical

consolidationists like Thaddeus Stevens and Henry Winter
Davis felt that the opportunity to fortify central authority and
establish its supremacy should be improved.

These were the ideas and principles of leading consolidationists and radicals in Congress who were politicians of ability,
had studied the science of government, and were from conviction opponents of reserved rights and State sovereignty and of a
mere confederation or Federal Union, based on the political
equality and reserved sovereignty of the States, but insisted that
the central Government should penetrate further and act directly on the people. Few of these had given much study or
thought to fundamental principles, the character and structure
of our Federal system, or the Constitution itself. Most of them,
under the pressure of schemers and enthusiasts, were willing to
assume and ready to exercise any power deemed expedient,
regardless of the organic law. Almost unrestrained legislation
to carry on the war induced a spirit of indifference to constitutional restraint, and brought about an assumption by some, a
belief by others, that Congress was omnipotent; that it was
the embodiment of the national will, and that the other departments of the Government as well as the States were subordinate and subject to central Congressional control. Absolute
power, the centralists assumed and their fanatical associates
seemed to suppose, was vested in the legislative body of the
country, and its decrees, arbitrary and despotic, often originating
in and carried first by a small vote in party caucus, were in all
cases claimed to be decisive, and to be obeyed by the Executive, the judiciary, and the people, regardless of the Constitution.
Parliamentary discussions were not permitted, or of little avail.
The acts of caucus were despotic, mandatory, and decisive. The
several propositions and plans of President Lincoln to reëstablish
the Union, and induce the seceding States to resume their
places and be represented in Congress, were received with disfavor by the radical leaders, who, without open assault, set in
motion an undercurrent against nearly every Executive proposition as the weak and impotent offspring of a well meaning
and well intentioned, but not very competent and intelligent

mind. It was the difference between President Lincoln and the radical leaders in Congress on the question of reconciliation, the restoration of the States, and the reëstablishment of the Union on the original constitutional basis, which more than even his genial and tolerant feelings toward the rebels led to political intrigue among Republican members of Congress for the nomination of new candidates, and opposition to Mr. Lincoln's reëlection in 1864. At one period this intrigue seemed formidable, and some professed friends lent it their countenance, if they did not actually participate in it, who ultimately disavowed any connection with the proceeding.

Singular ideas were entertained and began to be developed in propositions of an extraordinary character, relative to the powers and the construction of the Government, which were presented to Congress, even in the first year of the war. Theoretical schemes from cultivated intellects, as well as crude notions from less intellectual but extreme men, found expression in resolutions and plans, many of which were absurd and most of them impracticable and illegal. Foremost and prominent among them were a series of studied and elaborate resolutions prepared by Charles Sumner, and submitted to the Senate on the 11th of February, 1862. Although presented at that early day, they were the germ of the reconstruction policy adopted at a later period. In this plan or project for the treatment of the insurrectionary States and the people who resided in them, the Massachusetts Senator manifested little regard for the fundamental law or for State or individual rights. The high position which this Senator held in the Republican party and in Congress and the country, his cultured mind and scholarly attainments, his ardent if not always discreet zeal and efforts to free the slaves and endow the whole colored race, whether capable or otherwise, with all the rights and privileges, socially and politically, of the educated and refined white population whom they had previously served, his readiness and avowed intention to overthrow the local State governments and the social system where slavery existed, to subjugate the whites and elevate the blacks, will justify a special notice; for it was one of the first, if not the very first of the radical schemes officially presented to change the character of the Government and the previously existing distinctions between the races. His theory or plan may be taken as the pioneer of the many wild and visionary projects of the central and abolition force, that took shape and form not only during the war, but after hostilities ceased and the rebels were subdued.

Mr. Sumner introduced his scheme with a preamble which declared among other things, that the "extensive territory" of the South had been "usurped by pretended governments and organizations"; that "the Constitution, which is the supreme law of the land, cannot be displaced in its rightful operation within this territory, but must ever continue the supreme law thereof, notwithstanding the doings of any pretended governments acting singly or in confederation in order to put an end to its supremacy." Therefore:

> *Resolved,* 1st. That any vote of secession, or other act by which any State may undertake to put an end to the supremacy of the Constitution within its territory, is inoperative and void against the Constitution, and when sustained by force it becomes a practical *abdication* by the States of all rights under the Constitution, while the treason which it involves still further works an instant *forfeiture* of all those functions and powers essential to the continued existence of the State as a body politic, so that from that time forward the territory falls under the exclusive jurisdiction of Congress as other territory, and the State, being, according to the language of the law, *felo de se,* ceases to exist.
>
> 2d. That any combination of men assuming to act in the place of such State, attempting to ensnare or coerce the inhabitants thereof into a confederation hostile to the Union, is rebellious, treasonable, and destitute of all moral authority; and that such combination is a usurpation incapable of any constitutional existence and utterly lawless, so that everything dependent upon it is without constitutional or legal support.
>
> 3d. That the termination of a State under the Constitution necessarily causes the termination of those peculiar local institutions which, having no origin in the Constitu-

tion, or in those natural rights which exist independent of the Constitution, are upheld by the sole and exclusive authority of the State.

. . . Congress will assume complete jurisdiction of such vacated territory where such unconstitutional and illegal things have been attempted, and will proceed to establish therein republican forms of government under the Constitution.

It is not shown how a usurpation or illegal act by conspirators in any State or States could justify or make legal a usurpation by the general Government, as this scheme evidently was, nor by what authority Congress could declare that the illegal, inoperative, and void acts of usurpers who might have temporary possession of or be a majority in a State, could constitute a practical abdication by the State itself of all rights under the Constitution, regardless of the rights of a legal, loyal minority, guilty of no usurpation or attempted secession—the innocent victims of a conspiracy; nor where Congress or the Federal Government obtained authority to pronounce "an instant *forfeiture* of all those functions and powers essential to the continued existence of a State as a body politic, so that from that time forward the territory falls under the exclusive jurisdiction of Congress as other territory, and the State, being, according to the language of the law, *felo de se,* ceases to exist."

The administration of Mr. Buchanan had laid down as a rule of government that a State could not be coerced. The whole country not in rebellion had declared there should be no secession, division, or destruction of the Federal Union, but here was the most conspicuous leader of the Republican party in the Senate proposing a scheme to punish a State, to annihilate and destroy its government, to territorialize it, or exclude or expel it from the Union, to make no discrimination in its exclusions and denunciations between the loyal and disloyal inhabitants, but to punish alike, without trial or conviction, the just and the unjust. There were, though he was unwilling to admit it, and was perhaps unaware of it, vindictive feelings, venom, and revenge in his resolutions in his whole treatment of the States and the white people of the South. From the time that he had been stricken down by the bludgeon of Brooks in the Senate, Mr. Sumner waged unrelenting war on the whites in the Southern States, and seemed to suppose it was his special mission—he certainly made it the great object of his life—to elevate the negro race—to give them at least equal rights and privileges with the educated and refined class—and did not conceal his intention and expectation to bring them in as auxiliaries to the Republican party, and thereby give it permanent ascendancy. All this was done in the name of humanity, and with apparent self-convinced sincerity. He was unwilling to acknowledge that he was governed or influenced by personal resentments in his revolutionary plans to degrade the intelligent white and exalt the ignorant black population by tearing down the constitutional edifice. In frequent interviews which I held with him then and at later periods, when he found it impossible to hold his positions under the Constitutions, he claimed that he occupied higher ground, and that his authority for these violent measures was the Declaration of Independence, which declared all men were born equal, etc. Mr. Sumner was an idealist—neither a constitutionalist nor a practical statesman. He could pull down, but he could not construct—could declare what he considered humane, right, and proper, and act upon it regardless of constitutional compromises or conventional regulations which were the framework of the Government. No man connected with the Administration, or in either branch of Congress, was more thoroughly acquainted with our treaties, so familiar with the traditions of the Government, or better informed on international law than Charles Sumner; but on almost all other Governmental questions he was impulsive and unreliable, and when his feelings were enlisted, imperious, dogmatical, and often unjust.

Why innocent persons who were loyal to the Government and the Union should be disfranchised and proscribed because their neighbors and fellow citizens had engaged in a conspiracy, he could not explain or defend. By what authority whole communities and States should be deprived of the local governments which their fathers had framed, under which they were born, and with the provisions and traditions of which they were familiar, was never told.

His propositions found no favor with the Administration, nor were they supported at the beginning by any considerable number even of the extremists in Congress. It required much training by the centralizing leaders for years and all the tyranny of caucus machinery after the death of Mr. Lincoln to carry them into effect by a series of reconstruction measures that were revolutionary in their character, and which to a certain extent unsettled the principles on which the Government was founded.

But the counsel and example of the distinguished Senator from Massachusetts were not without their influence. Resolutions by radical Republicans and counter resolutions, chiefly by Democrats, relative to the powers and limitations of the Federal Government and the status of States, followed in quick succession. On the 11th of June, the subject having been agitated and discussed for four months, Mr. Dixon, a Republican Senator from Connecticut, whose views coincided in the main with those of Mr. Lincoln and the Administration, submitted, after consultation and advisement, the following:

> *Resolved,* That all acts or ordinances of secession, alleged to have been adopted by any legislation or convention of the people of any State, are as to the Federal Union absolutely null and void; and that while such acts may and do subject the individual actors therein to forfeitures and penalties, they do not, in any degree, affect the relations of the State wherein they purport to have been adopted to the Government of the United States, but are as to such Government acts of rebellion, insurrection, and hostility on the part of the individuals engaged therein, or giving assent thereto; and that such States are, notwithstanding such acts or ordinances, members of the Federal Union, and as such are subject to all the obligations and duties imposed upon them by the Constitution of the United States; and the loyal citizens of such States are entitled to all the rights and privileges thereby guaranteed or conferred.

The resolution of Dixon traversed the policy of Sumner and was the Executive view of the questions that were agitated in Congress as to the effect of the rebellion and the condition of the States in insurrection. The Administration did not admit that rebellion dissolved the Union or destroyed its federative character; nor did it adopt or assent to the novel theory that the States and the whole people residing in them had forfeited all sovereignty and all reserved State and individual rights, because a portion of the inhabitants had rebelled; nor did it admit that the usurpation of a portion of any community could bring condemnation and punishment on all. The usurpations and acts of the rebels were considered not legal acts, but nullities.

4

Administration of Abraham Lincoln, II

In his management of the Republican party, Abraham
Lincoln was confronted by a serious split between radicals and conservatives. While the radicals were in favor
of immediate emancipation and far-reaching changes
in the Southern States, the conservatives tended to
deprecate hasty actions and emphasize the preservation
of the Union. In the following essay, Welles discusses
the origins of this split.

THE SECOND SESSION of the Thirty-seventh Congress,
from its commencement to its close, tested the strength of the
Government and the capability of those who administered it.
Disappointment, in consequence of no decisive military success
during the first few months of the war, had caused a generally
depressed feeling which begot discontent and distrust that in
various ways found expression in Congress. Democrats complained more of the incapacity of the Executive than of the inefficiency of the generals, and the entire Administration was
censured and denounced by them for acts which, if not strictly
legal and constitutional in peace, were necessary and unavoid-
able in war. Republicans, on the other hand, were dissatisfied
because so little was accomplished, and the factious imputed
military delay to mismanagement and want of energy in the
Administration. Indeed, but for some redeeming naval successes
at Hatteras and Port Royal preceding the meeting of Congress
in December, the whole belligerent operations would have been

The Galaxy, XXIII (February, 1877).

pronounced weak and imbecile failures. Conflicting views in regard to the slavery question in all its aspects prevailed; the Democrats insisting that fugitives should be returned to their masters under the provisions of law, as in time of peace. The Republicans were divided on this question, one portion agreeing with the Democrats that all should be returned, another claiming that only escaped slaves who belonged to loyal owners, wherever they resided, should be returned; another portion insisted that there should be no rendition of servants of rebel masters, even in loyal or border States, who, by resisting the laws and setting the authorities at defiance, had forfeited their rights and all Governmental protection. Questions in regard to the treatment of captured rebels, and the confiscation of all property of rebels, were agitated. What was the actual condition of the seceding States, and what would be their status when the rebellion should be suppressed, were also beginning to be controverted points, especially among members of Congress. On these and other questions which the insurrection raised, novel, perplexing, and without law or precedent to guide or govern it, the Administration had developed no well defined policy when Congress convened in December, 1861, but it was compelled to act, and that in such a manner as not to alienate friends or give unnecessary offence, while maintaining the Government in all its Federal authority and rights for the preservation of the Union and the suppression of the rebellion.

The character and duration of the war, which many had supposed would be brief, was still undetermined. While affairs were in this uncertain and inchoate condition, and the Administration had no declared policy on some of the most important questions, Congress came together fired with indignation and revenge for a war so causeless and unprovoked. A large portion of the members, exasperated toward the rebels by reason of the war, and dissatisfied with delays and procrastination, which they imputed chiefly to the Administration, were determined there should be prompt and aggressive action against the persons, property, institutions, and the States which had confederated to break up the Union. There was, however, little unity among the complaining members as to the mode and method

of prosecuting the war. It was not difficult to find fault with
the Administration, but it was not easy for the discontented to
settle on any satisfactory plan of continuing it. The Democrats
complained that the President transcended his rightful authority;
the radical portion of the Republicans that he was not sufficiently aggressive; that he was deficient in energy and too tender
of the rebels. It was at this period, after Congress had been
in session two months, and opinions were earnest but diverse and
factious, with a progeny of crude and mischievous schemes as to
the conduct of affairs and the treatment of the rebels, that
Senator Sumner, in the absence of a clearly defined policy on
the part of the Administration, and while things were not sufficiently matured to adopt one, submitted his project for overthrowing the State governments and reducing them to a territorial condition, and with the subversion of their governments
the abolition of slavery. It was the enunciation of a policy that
was in conflict with the Constitution, and would change the
character of the Government, but which he intended to force
upon the Administration. Though a scheme devised by himself,
it had in its main features the countenance of many and some
able supporters.

President Lincoln had high respect for Mr. Sumner, but was
excessively annoyed with this presentation of the extreme, and,
as he considered them, unconstitutional and visionary theories
of the Massachusetts Senator, which were intended to commit
the Government and shape its course. It was precipitating upon
the Administration issues on delicate and deeply important subjects at a critical period—issues involving the structure of the
Government and the stability of our Federal system. These
questions might have to be ultimately met and disposed of, but it
was requisite that they should be met with caution and deliberate consideration. The times and condition of the country were
inauspicious for considerate statesmanship. The matters in dispute, the consequences and results of the war, were yet in
embryo. There could be no union of sentiment on Senator
Sumner's plan, nor any other at that period, in the free States,
in Congress, or even in the Republican party. There were half
a dozen factions to be reconciled or persuaded to act together.

This plan was felt to be an element of discord, which, if it could not be finally averted, might in that gloomy period, when the country was threatened and divided, have been temporarily, at least, avoided. But Senator Sumner, though scholarly and cultured, was not always judicious or wisely discreet. The President, as he expressed himself, could not, in the then condition of affairs, afford to have a controversy with Sumner, but he so managed as to check violent and aggressive demands by quietly interposing delay and non-action.

In the mean time, while the subjects of slavery, reconstruction, and confiscation were being vehemently discussed, he felt the necessity of adopting, or at least proposing, some measure to satisfy public sentiment.

On the subject of confiscation there were differing opinions among the Republicans themselves, in Congress, which called out earnest debate. The Radicals, such as Thaddeus Stevens, who were in fact revolutionists and intended that more should be accomplished by the Government than the suppression of the rebellion and the preservation of the Union, were for the immediate and unsparing confiscation of the property of the rebels by act of Congress without awaiting judicial proceedings. In their view and by their plan rebels, if not outlaws, were to be considered and treated as foreigners, not as American citizens; the States in insurrection were to be reduced to the condition of provinces; the people were to be subjugated and their property taken to defray the expenses of the war. Mr. Sumner, less crafty and calculating than Stevens, but ardent and impulsive, was for proceeding to extreme lengths; and, having the power, he urged that they should embrace "the opportunity which God in his beneficence had offered" to extinguish by arbitrary enactment slavery, and all claim to reserved sovereignty in the States; but Judge Collamer, calm and considerate, and other milder men were opposed to any illegal and unjustifiable enactment.

As is too often the case in high party and revolutionary times, the violent and intriguing were likely to be successful, until it came to be understood that the President would feel it obligatory to place upon the extreme and unconstitutional measures his veto. A knowledge of this and the attending fact, that his veto would be sustained, induced Congress to pass a joint resolution, modifying the act, expounding and declaring its meaning, instead of enacting a new and explicit law, which the judiciary, whose province it is, would expound and construe.

The President, in order not to be misunderstood when informing the House of Representatives that he had affixed his signature to the bill and joint resolution, also transmitted a copy of the message he had prepared to veto the act in its original shape, with his objections, in which he said that by a fair construction of the act he considered persons "are not punished without regular trials, in duly constituted courts, under the forms and the substantial provisions of the law and the Constitution applicable to their several cases." It was apprehended at that time, and subsequent acts proved the apprehension well founded, that Congress or its radical leaders were disposed to assume and exercise not only legislative, but judicial and executive powers. Rebels were by Congress to be condemned and their property confiscated and taken without trial and conviction. Such was not the policy of the President, as was soon well understood; and to reconcile him and those who agreed with him, a provision was inserted that persons who should commit treason and be *"adjudged guilty thereof"* should be punished. But to prevent misconception from equivocal phraseology in a somewhat questionable act, he explicitly made known that "regular trials in duly constituted courts" were to be observed, and the rights of the executive and judicial departments of the Government maintained. This precaution, and the determination which he uniformly expressed to regard individual rights, and not to impose penalty or inflict punishment for alleged crimes, whether of treason or felony, until after trial and conviction, was not satisfactory to the extremists, who were ready to treat rebels as outlaws, and condemn them without judge or jury.

The Centralists in Congress, who were arrogating executive and judicial as well as legislative power, authorized the President, by special provision in this law, to extend pardon and amnesty on such occasions as he might deem expedient. This was represented as special grace and a great concession; but as the pardoning power is explicitly conferred on the President by the Constitution, the permission or authorization given by the act was entirely supererogatory. Congress could neither enlarge nor diminish the authority of the Executive in that respect; but if the President acquiesced, and admitted the right of the legislative body to grant, it was evident the day was not distant that the same body, when dissatisfied with his leniency, would claim the right to restrain or prohibit. The ulterior design in this grant to the President of authority which he already possessed, and of which they could not legally deprive him, President Lincoln well understood, but felt it to be his duty and it was his policy to have as little controversy with Congress or any of the factions in that body as was possible, and he therefore wisely forebore contention.

On the slavery question, the alleged cause of secession and war, there were legal and perplexing difficulties which, in various ways, embarrassed the Administration, and in the disturbed condition of the country prevented, for a time, the establishment and enforcement of any decisive policy. By the Constitution and laws, slavery and property in slaves were recognized, and the surrender and rendition of fugitives from service to their owners was commanded; but in a majority of the seceding States the usurping governments and the rebel slave-owners were in open insurrection, resisting the Federal authority, defying it and making war upon it. Still there were many citizens in those States who were opposed to secession, loyal to the Federal Government, and earnest friends of the Union, who owned slaves. What policy could the Administration adopt in regard to these two classes of citizens in the same State? The fugitive slave law was not and could not be enforced in States where there was organized rebellion. Should fugitive slaves be returned to both, or either, or neither of the owners in insurrectionary States? There were moreover five or six border States, where slavery existed, which did not secede. The governments and a majority of the people of those states were patriotic supporters of the Union, but there was a large minority in each of them who were violent enemies of the Government and of the Union. Many of them were serving in the rebel armies. For a time there was no alternative but to return slaves to their owners who resided in border States which had neither seceded nor resisted the Government. The Administration was not authorized to discriminate, for instance, between slave-owners on the eastern shore of the Potomac in the lower counties of Maryland and those on the western shore in Virginia. There were, however, no secessionists, through the whole South, more malignantly hostile to the Federal Union than a large portion of the slave-owners in the southern counties of Maryland; but the State not having seceded, and there being no organized resistance to the Government, masters who justified secession continued to reclaim their slaves, while on the opposite side of the river, in Virginia, slave-owners who claimed to be loyal or neutral, could not reclaim or obtain a restoration of their escaped servants. The Executive was compelled to act in each of these cases, and its policy, the dictate of necessity in the peculiar war that existed, was denounced by each of the disagreeing factions. Affairs were in this unsettled and broken condition when Congress convened at its second session in December, 1861. The action of the President in these conflicting cases as they arose, if not condemned, was not fully approved. Many, if not a majority, in Congress were determined what course to take. Democrats insisted that the laws must be obeyed in all cases, in war as in peace. The radical portion of the Republicans began to take extreme opposite grounds, and claim that the laws were inoperative in regard to slavery—that slavery was at all times inconsistent with a republican government, and should now be extinguished. Among the revolutionary resolutions of Senator Sumner of the 11th of February were some on the subject of slavery. Other but not dissimilar propositions, antagonistic to slavery, found expression, increasing in intensity as the war was prolonged. While it was evident to most persons that one of the results of the insurrection would be, in some way or form, the emancipation of the slaves, there was no person who seemed capable of devising a constitutional, practical plan for its accomplishment, except by subjugation and violence. To these the

President was unwilling to resort; yet the necessity of doing something that did not transcend the law, was morally right, and would tend to the ultimate freedom of the slaves was felt to be an essential and indispensable duty. Unavailing but seductive appeals continued in the mean time to be made by the secessionists to the people of the border slave States to unite with the further South for the security and protection of slavery, in which they had a common interest, and against which there was increasing hostility through the North. It was under these circumstances, with a large and growing portion of the North in favor of abolition—the slave States, including the border States, opposed to the measure and for the preservation of the institution—that the President was to prescribe a policy on which the government in the disordered state of the country was to be administered.

To surmount the difficulties, without setting aside the law, or giving just offence to any, the President, with his accustomed prudence and regard for existing legal rights, devised a course which, if acquiesced in by those most in interest, would, he believed, in a legal way open the road to ultimate, if not immediate, emancipation. Instead of assenting to the demands of the radical extremists that he should, by arbitary proceedings, and in disregard of law and Constitution, decree freedom to all slaves, he preferred milder and more conciliatory measures. The authority or right of the national Government to abolish or interfere with an institution that was reserved and belonged exclusively to the States, he was not prepared to act upon or admit, though entreated and urged thereto by sincere party friends, and also by party supporters, whose sincerity was doubtful.

There could be no excuse or pretext for such interference but the insurrection; and even as a war measure, there were obstacles in the condition of the border slave States, to say nothing of loyal, patriotic citizens in the insurrectionary region, that could not be overlooked.

On the 6th of March, within less than three weeks after Senator Sumner had submitted his revolutionary resolution, for reconstruction, and a declaration that it is the duty of Con-

gress "to see that everywhere in this extensive (secession) territory slavery shall cease to exist practically, as it has already
ceased to exist constitutionally or morally," that President Lincoln, not assenting to the assumption, sent a message to Congress proposing a plan of voluntary and compensated emancipation. In this message he suggested that "the United States
ought to co-operate with any State which may adopt gradual
abolishment of slavery, giving to each State pecuniary aid,"
etc., and he invited an interview upon the 10th of March,
with the representatives of the border States, to consider the
subject. They did not conclude at this interview to adopt his
suggestions, and some of them were much incensed that the
proposition had been made, believing it would alienate and
drive many, hitherto rightly disposed, into secession.

Nevertheless, the fact that slavery was doomed, and had
received a death blow from the war of secession, was so obvious, that the moderate and reflecting began seriously to consider whether they ought not to give the President's plan
favorable consideration.

While the policy of voluntary emancipation, in which the
States should be aided by the national Government, was not
immediately successful, it made such advance as, by the aid
of the Federal Government, led to the abolition of slavery in
the District of Columbia. The advocates of immediate, general, and forcible emancipation, if not satisfied with the conciliatory policy of the President, could not well oppose it.

Warm discussions in Congress, and altercations out of it,
on most of the important questions growing out of the war,
and particularly on those of confiscation, emancipation, and
reconstruction, or the restoration of the States to their rightful
position, and the reëstablishment of the Union, were had during the whole of the second session of the Thirty-seventh Congress. All of these were exciting and important questions, the
last involving grave principles affecting our federal system,
and was most momentous in its consequences. As time and events
passed on, the convictions and conclusions of the President became more clear and distinct as to the line of policy which
it was his duty and that of the Administration to pursue.

Dissenting, wholly and absolutely, from the revolutionary views and schemes of Senator Sumner and those who agreed with him, the President became convinced, as the subject had been prematurely introduced and agitated, with an evident intent to forestall and shape the action of the Government, that the actual status of the rebel States and their true relation to the Federal Government should be distinctly understood. The resolution of Mr. Dixon, a gentleman of culture and intelligence, who, as well as Mr. Sumner, was a New England Senator, and also of the same party, was, it will be observed, diametrically opposed to the principles and the project of the Massachusetts Senator on the great, impending, and forthcoming subject of reconstruction. It was directly known that the President coincided with the Connecticut Senator in the opinion that all the acts and ordinances of secession were mere nullities, and should be so treated; that while such acts might subject *individuals* to penalties and forfeitures, they did not in any degree affect the *States* as commonwealths, and their relations to the Federal Government; that such acts were rebellious, insurrectionary, and hostile on the part of the *persons* engaged in them, but that the *States,* notwithstanding the acts and conspiracies of individuals, were still members of the Federal Union, and that the loyal citizens of these States had forfeited none of their rights, but were entitled to all the protection and privileges guaranteed by the Constitution.

The theory and principles set forth in Senator Dixon's resolutions were the opinions and convictions of the President, deliberately formed and consistently maintained while he lived, on the subject of reconstruction and the condition of the States and people in the insurrectionary region. In his view there was no actual secession, no dismembering of the Union, no change in the Constitution and Government; the relative position of the States and the Federal Government were unchanged; the organic, fundamental laws of neither were altered by the sectional conspiracy; the whole people, North and South, were American citizens; each person was responsible for his own acts and amenable to law; and he was also entitled to the protection of the law, and the rights and privileges secured by the Con-

stitution. The confiscation and emancipation schemes concerning
which there was so much excitement in Congress were of secondary consideration to the all-absorbing one of preserving the
Union.

The second session of the Thirty-seventh Congress closed
on the 17th of July. Its proceedings had been confused and
uneasy, with a good deal of discontented and revolutionary
feeling, which increased toward the close. The decisive stand
which the President had taken, and which he calmly, firmly,
and persistently maintained against the extreme measures of
some of the most prominent Republicans in Congress, was unsatisfactory. It was insinuated that his sympathies on important
measures had more of a Democratic than Republican tendency;
yet the Democratic party maintained an organized and often
unreasonable, if not unpatriotic, opposition.

Military operations, aside from naval success at New Orleans
and on the upper Mississippi, had been a succession of military
reverses. Disagreement between the Secretary of War and the
General-in-Chief, which the President could not reconcile,
caused the latter to be superseded after the disastrous result before Richmond. Dissensions in the army and among the Republicans in Congress, the persistent opposition of Democrats
to the Administration and the general depression that prevailed
were discouraging. "In my position," said the President, "I
am environed with difficulties." Friends on whom he felt he
ought to be able to rely were dissatisfied with his conscientious
scruples and lenity, and party opponents were unrelenting
against the Administration.

A few days before Congress adjourned, the President made
another but unsuccessful effort to dispose of the slavery question, by trying to induce the border States to take the initiative
in his plan of compensated emancipation. The interview between him and the representatives of the border States, which
took place on the 12th of July, convinced him that the project
of voluntary emancipation by the States would not succeed.
Were it commenced by one or more of the States, he had little
doubt it would be followed by others, and eventuate in general
emancipation by the States themselves. Failing in the voluntary

plan, he was compelled, as a war necessity, to proclaim freedom to all slaves in the rebel section, if the war continued to be prosecuted after a certain date. This bold and almost revolutionary measure, which would change the industrial character of many States, could be justified on no other ground than as a war measure, the result of military necessity. It was an unexpected and startling demonstration when announced, that was welcomed by a vast majority of the people in the free States. In Congress, however, neither this nor his project of compensated emancipation was entirely acceptable to either the extreme anti-slavery or pro-slavery men. The radicals disliked the way in which emancipation was effected by the President. But, carried forward by the force of public opinion, they could not do otherwise than acquiesce in the decree, complaining, however, that it was an unauthorized assumption by the Executive of power which belonged to Congress.

The opponents of the President seized the occasion of this bold measure to create distrust and alarm, and the result of the policy of emancipation in the election which followed in the autumn of 1862 was adverse to the Administration. Confident, however, that the step was justifiable and necessary, the President persevered and consummated it by a final proclamation on the 1st of January, 1863.

The fact that the Administration lost ground in the elections in consequence of the emancipation policy served for a time to promote unity of feeling among the members when Congress convened in December. The shock occasioned by the measure when first announced had done its work. The timid, who had doubted the necessity and legality of the act, and feared its consequences, recovered their equipoise, and a reaction followed which strengthened the President in public confidence. But the radical extremists, especially the advocates of Congressional supremacy, began in the course of the winter to reassert their own peculiar ideas and their intention of having a more extreme policy pursued by the Government.

Thaddeus Stevens embraced an early opportunity to declare his extreme views, which were radically and totally antagonistic to those of the President. But Stevens, whose ability and acquirements as a politician, and whose skill and experience as a party tactician were unsurpassed if not unequalled in either branch of Congress, made no open, hostile demonstration toward the President. He restricted himself to contemptuous expressions in private conversation against the Executive policy and general management of affairs. Without an attack on the President, whom he personally liked, the Administration was sneered at as weak and inefficient, of which little could be expected until a more aggressive and scathing policy was adopted. His personal intercourse with members and his talents and eloquence on the floor of the House gave him influence with the representatives on ordinary occasions, but his ultra radical and revolutionary ideas caused the calm and considerate to distrust and disclaim his opinions and his leadership. It was not until a later period, and under another Executive, less affable but not less honest and sincere than Mr. Lincoln, that the suggestions of Stevens were much regarded. When his disciples and adherents became more partisan and numerous, they, in order to give him power and consequence and reconcile their constituents, denominated him the "Great Commoner."

If his political hopes and party schemes had been sometimes successful, his reverses and disappointments had been much greater. Many and severe trials during an active, embittered, and often unscrupulous partisan experience, had tempered his enthusiasm if they had not brought him wisdom. Defeats can hardly be said to have made him misanthropic; but having little philosophy in his composition, he vented his spleen when there was occasion on his opponents in ironical remarks that made him dreaded, and which were often more effective than arguments; but his sagacity and knowledge of men taught him that a hostile and open conflict with a chief magistrate whose honesty even he respected, and whose patriotism the people so generally regarded, would be not only unavailing, but to himself positively injurious. He therefore conformed to circumstances; and while opposed to the tolerant policy of the Administration toward the rebels and the rebel States, he had the tact and address, with his wit and humor, to preserve pleasant social intercourse and friendly personal relations with the President, who well understood his traits and purpose, but avoided any conflict with him.

For the first five or six weeks of the third session of the Thirty-seventh Congress, Stevens improved his time in free and sarcastic remarks on the reconstruction policy of the Government, which he characterized as puerile and feeble, and at length, on the 8th of January, he gave utterance to his feelings, maintaining that "with regard to all the Southern States in rebellion, the Constitution has no binding influence or application." He averred that "in his opinion they were not members of the Union"; that "the ordinances of secession took them out of the Union"; that he "would levy a tax wherever he could upon these conquered provinces"; said he "would not only collect the tax, but he would, as a necessary war measure, take every particle of property, real and personal, life estate and reversion, of every disloyal man, and sell it for the benefit of the nation in carrying on this war."

Several members of Congress hastened to deny that these sentiments and purposes were those of the Republican party; this Mr. Stevens admitted. He said "a very mild denial from the pleasant gentleman from New York [Mr. Olin], and the somewhat softened and modified repudiation of the gentleman from Indiana" [Mr. Colfax], would, he hoped, satisfy the sensitive gentlemen in regard to him, and he "desired to say he did not speak the sentiments of this side of the House *as a party";* that "for the last fifteen years he [Stevens] had always been ahead of the party in these matters, but he had never been so far ahead but that the members of the party had overtaken and gone ahead; and they would again overtake him and go with him before the infamous and bloody rebellion was ended." "They will find that they must treat those States, now outside of the Union, as conquered provinces, and settle them with new men, and drive the present rebels as exiles from this country." "Nothing but extermination, or exile, or starvation, will ever induce them to surrender to the Government."

Not very consistent or logical in his policy and views, this subsequently Radical leader proposed to treat the Southern people sometimes as foreigners and at other times as rebel citizens; in either case he would tax, starve, and exile them—make provinces of their States, and overturn their old established governments. Few, comparatively, of the Republicans were at that time prepared to follow Stevens or adopt his vindictive and arbitrary measures. Shocked at his propositions, the "Great Commoner" had at that day few acknowledged adherents. When in vindication of his scheme it was asked upon what ground the collection of taxes could be enforced in the Southern States, Judge Thomas, one of the ablest and clearest minds of the Massachusetts delegation, said, "Upon this ground, that the authority of this Government at this time is as valid over those States as it was before the acts of secession were passed; upon the ground that every act of secession passed by those States is utterly null and void; upon the ground that every act legally null and void cannot acquire force because armed rebellion is behind it, seeking to uphold it; upon the ground that the Constitution makes us not a mere confederacy, but a *nation;* upon the ground that the provisions of that Constitution strike through the State government and reach directly, not intermediately, the subjects. Subjects of whom? Of the nation—of the United States." "Who ever heard, as a matter of public law, that the authority of a government over its rebellious subjects was lost until that revolution was successful—was a fact accomplished?"

Shortly after the capture of New Orleans and the establishment of Federal authority over Louisiana, two of the Congressional districts of that State elected representatives to Congress. The admission or non-admission of these representatives involved the question of the political condition of the Southern States and people in the Federal Union, and the whole principle, in fact, of restoration and reconstruction.

The subject was long and deliberately considered and fully discussed in Congress. The committee on elections reported in favor of their admission, and Mr. Dawes of Massachusetts, the chairman, stated that "more than ordinary importance is attached to the consideration of this subject. It is not simply whether two gentlemen shall be permitted to occupy seats in this House. The question whether they shall be admitted in-

volves the principles touching the present state of the country
to which the attention of the House has more than once been
called." He said, "The question now comes up, whether any
reason exists that requires any departure from the rules and
principles which have been adopted." "An adherence to these
principles is vitally important in settling the question, how
there is to be a restoration of this Union when this war shall
be drawn to a close."

The subject of admitting these representatives and the principles of a restoration of the Union which their admission involved, was debated with earnestness for several days, and finally
decided, on the 17th of February, in favor of admitting them,
by a vote of ninety-two in the affirmative to forty-four in the
negative.

An analysis of this vote, in view of the proceedings, acts, and
votes of many of the same members a few years subsequently,
after Mr. Lincoln's death, presents some curious and interesting
facts. It was not a strictly party vote. Among those who then
favored the Administration policy of restoration were Colfax,
Dawes, Delano, Fenton, Fisher of Delaware, Wm. Kellogg, J. S.
Morrill of Vermont, Governor A. H. Rice of Massachusetts,
Shellabarger, and others who opposed the restoration policy of
President Lincoln after his death and the accession of President
Johnson.

In the negative with Thaddeus Stevens were Ashley, Bing-
ham, the two Conklings, Kelley, McPherson, and a few others.
But when reconstruction or exclusion actually took place after
the termination of the war, great changes occurred among the
members of Congress, and Stevens, the "Great Commoner,"
who in 1863 had a following of less than one-third of the representatives, rallied, four years later, more than two-thirds to his
standard against restoration and for subjugation and exclusion.

Mr. Stevens was no ordinary man. At the bar he was astute
and eloquent rather than profound, but in the Legislature of
Pennsylvania and in the management of the affairs of that
State, where for a period he actively participated and was a
ruling mind, he was often rash and turbulent, and had, not
without cause, the reputation of being a not over scrupulous

politician. Personally my relations with him, though not intimate, were pleasant and friendly. I was first introduced to him
at Harrisburg in 1836, when he was a member of the convention
that revised the Constitution of Pennsylvania. We occasionally
met in after years. He expressed himself pleased with my appointment in Mr. Lincoln's Cabinet, and, notwithstanding we
disagreed on fundamental principles, he complimented my administration of the Navy Department, and openly and always
sustained my positions, and particularly so on the subject of the
blockade, on which there were differences in the Administration.
In the Pennsylvania convention of 1836 he was probably the
most eloquent speaker, but his ideas were often visionary and
radical. He ultimately refused to sign the Constitution because
the colored people were denied the elective franchise. Severe
as he exhibited himself toward the rebels during and subsequent
to the civil war, Mr. Stevens was not by nature, as might be
supposed, inhuman in his feelings and sympathies toward his
fellow men. To the colored race he seemed always more attached and tender than to the whites, perhaps because they
were enslaved and oppressed. He was opposed to slavery, to
imprisonment for debt, and to capital punishment. There were
strange contradictions in his character. In his political career
he had ardent supporters, though many who voted with him
had not a high regard for his principles. His course and conduct
in the Legislature and government of Pennsylvania did much
to debauch the political morals of that State, and in the cele-
brated "buck-shot war" he displayed the bold and reckless disregard of justice and popular rights that distinguished the latter
years of his Congressional life, when he became the acknowledged
leader of the radical reconstruction party in Congress.

In his political career and management, though strongly
sustained by a local constituency, he had experienced a series
of disappointments. The defeat of John Quincy Adams, whom
he greatly admired, in 1828, and the election of General Jackson, against whom his prejudices were inveterate, were to him
early and grievous vexations.

The attempt of Mr. Adams on his retirement to establish
a national anti-Masonic party was warmly seconded by Stevens,

and with greater success in Pennsylvania than attended his distinguished leader in Massachusetts. The failure of the attempt was more severely felt by the disciple than by the master. After the annihilation of the anti-Masonic organization and the discomfiture of the buck-shot war, Stevens was less conspicuous, though prominent for a few months in 1840, when he came forward as an earnest advocate of the nomination of General Harrison in that singular campaign which resulted in the General's election. His efficiency and zeal in behalf of both the nomination and election of the "hero of Tippecanoe" were acknowledged, and he and his friends anticipated they would be recognized and be rewarded by a seat in the Cabinet. But he had given offence to the great Whig leader of that day by his preference of Harrison for President, and had moreover an unsavory reputation, which, with the declared opposition of Clay and Webster, caused his exclusion. It was a sore disappointment, from which he never fully recovered. Eight years later, with the advent of General Taylor and the defeated aspirations of the Whig leaders, who had caused his exclusion from Harrison's Cabinet, he sought and obtained an election to the thirty-first Congress from the Lancaster district. In 1856 he strove with all his power to secure the Presidential nomination for John McLane of the Supreme Court, who had or professed to have had anti-Masonic tendencies. His ill success was another disappointment; but in 1859 he was again elected to Congress, and thereafter until his death he represented the Lancaster district.

Disappointments had made him splenetic, but he was not, as represented by his opponents on the two extremes, either a charlatan or a miscreant, though possible not wholly exempt from charges against him in either respect. In many of his ultra-radical and it may be truly said revolutionary views—revolutionary because they changed the structure of the Government—he coincided with Senator Sumner, who was perhaps the leading spirit in the State on the subject of reconstruction, but he did not, like the Massachusetts Senator, make any pretence that his project to subjugate the Southern people and reduce their States to the condition of provinces was constitutional, or by authority of the Declaration of Independence. President Lincoln well understood the characteristics of both these men, and, though differing from each on the subject of restoration and reconstruction, he managed to preserve personal relations with both—retained their confidence, and while he lived secured their general support of his Administration. Herein President Lincoln exhibited those peculiar qualities and attributes of mind which made him a leader and manager of men, and enabled him in a quiet and unostentatious way to exercise his executive ability in administering the Government during the most troublesome period of our national history.

5

Administration of Abraham Lincoln, III

What to do with the emancipated Negroes became one of the major problems confronting the Lincoln Administration. In this essay, Welles examines Lincoln's attitude toward abolition, reconstruction, and colonization, with interesting references to the persistent rivalry between Secretaries Seward and Chase.

RECONSTRUCTION, as it was called, the desire for the restoration, preservation, and perpetuation of the Union, was a matter of absorbing interest, which began almost with the war, and was mingled with all public measures from the commencement of hostilities. The questions affecting the character and structure of the Government were the matters of political controversy long after the armies were disbanded and hostilities had ceased. The civil war, its effect upon our political system, and what would be the condition of the country at its close, brought out the distinctive political principles of the opposing parties which, under various names and phases, had agitated the country from the foundation of the Government. In the necessary exercise of war power to suppress the rebellion those who favored a strong, central, supervisory national government were strengthened in their opinions by the extraordinary measures adopted, while the Statists, who opposed centralism and consolidation, and were for limiting the national government to national questions and the exercise of only the powers specified and granted in the Constitution, were for the moment corres-

The Galaxy, XXIV (October, 1877).

pondingly weakened. But a strict construction of the Constitution, and a rigid adherence to its provisions, as in time of peace, were insufficient for an energetic prosecution of measures to overcome the powerful, organized, armed resistance to the Government. An avowed sectional combination to dismember the Union had sprung up, and was supported by the State authorities South, and no inconsiderable portion of the thorough party men, who had been trained against centralism, opposed governmental proceedings, which were the result of military necessity, and absolutely essential to sustain the national existence. Those who were enlisted in this section combination had not voted for Abraham Lincoln, and they, and many of their Northern political associates and sympathizers, would not as a party support his administration. On the other hand, a class of extreme centralists, unwilling to submit to the restraints of the organic law, and who had about as much reverence for the Constitution as for the resolutions of a political party convention, were not satisfied that the President and his advisers refused to exercise absolute power, or hesitated to assume, in such an exigency, authority not specifically delegated. One class of extremists claimed the President transcended his rightful authority, and did too much; another class insisted that in his war measures he was inefficient, and did too little. Neither extreme controlled the Executive. It was impossible, with good administration, to adapt or assent to the impulsive demands of the radicals and it would have been dereliction and abandonment of duty on the other hand to have acquiesced in the passive, non-combative, peace doctrine of the ultra Northern Democrats in the midst of a formidable and organized rebellion.

The progress of events wrought changes of opinion, and influenced the action of the Administration. Emancipation had constituted no part of the policy of the President at the time of his inauguration, and when finally decreed he connected with it, as an essential and indispensable part of his policy, a plan of deportation of the colored population. Long before he yielded to emancipation, and in the belief that it was necessary to rid the country of the African race, he had schemes for their migration more advanced than those of the colonizationists.

From a conviction that the white and black races could not abide together on terms of social and political equality, he thought they could not peaceably occupy the same territory— that one must dominate the other. Opposed to the whole system of enslavement, but believing the Africans were mentally an inferior race, he believed that any attempt to make them and the whites one people would tend to the degradation of the whites without materially elevating the blacks, but that separation would promote the happiness and welfare of each. In this view he was not singular, even among anti-slavery men. Henry Clay, the life-long leader of the party with which Mr. Lincoln had been associated in early life, was an active colonizationist, and his views contributed no doubt to the President's scheme of deportation as an indispensable accompaniment of emancipation.

In May, 1861, the President had made known his opinions on this subject of deportation and colonization, and his belief that some suitable and inviting territory within the tropics, less remote than Africa, might be obtained, to which the colored people could be induced to migrate. Aware of his feelings and views, an association of gentlemen, who claimed to have acquired a title to the territory of Chiriqui in Central America, urged that the Government should purchase the grant and make it available for a colored settlement. The President was much taken with the suggestion, and it was warmly advocated by several members of the Cabinet. He referred the proposition to me, with his favorable endorsement, to investigate and report on its practicability. The examination which I made after this reference did not favorably impress me as to the purchase or the policy. There had been under the preceding administration a project to obtain this Chiriqui grant, not for African colonization, but ostensibly for the purpose of securing for naval purposes a harbor and alleged inexhaustible quantities of coal at a commanding point of the Caribbean sea and the Gulf of Mexico. A naval vessel, under Commodore Engle, had been sent thither by Secretary Toucey, with engineers, to explore the country, examine its topographical and hydrographical features, and ascertain the quality of coal reputed to be there in abundance, and of a superior quality. Their reports were highly favorable, but before the arrangements for the acquisition of the grant were completed a change of administration took place. The parties in interest brought forward the subject of this purchase, in 1861, to the new administration, coupled with a scheme of African or colored colonization. The deported negroes, it was represented, could be advantageously employed in mining coal. The whole project had to me the appearance of a speculative job, into which the preceding administration had been seduced. I reported to the President that I had no faith in the project; that the Navy Department had other duties than those of colonizing negroes and mining coal, even if coal were there; that the Chiriqui territory presented no inducements for the colored race to emigrate thither; that if the negroes were there, they would not willingly work, nor were mining labors and operations congenial to them. The whole scheme, though skill-fully presented in the name of humanity, had a money-making appearance in the interest of not over scrupulous speculators; further than that, I had never been favorable to the plan of African colonization by the Government. Differing as I did from him and others on the question, it would be proper that the subject, if to be prosecuted, should be committed to some member of the Cabinet who was otherwise impressed.

The papers were then handed to Mr. Caleb Smith, Secretary of the Interior, an earnest colonizationist, who ardently advocated the Chiriqui project. He promptly recommended the purchaser the immediate settlement of a black colony there, and that the Navy Department should make an advance of $50,000 toward its acquisition, to be repaid in coal, which the colonists would furnish for our squadrons. There ought, he reported, to be no delay in securing the grant, for both the English and French were anxious to obtain it, and would already have purchased it but for the patriotism of the proprietors, who preferred that this important station in Costa Rica should come into possession of the American Government. Smith's report was plausibly presented, and the President approved it without himself investigating the legality of the title, which he took for granted had been attended to by both Mr. Smith and the Buchanan administration, which had introduced the measure and favored the purchase. Most of the Cabinet assented. Both Mr. Bates and Mr. Blair were colonizationists, and in favor of deportation. Mr. Chase and Mr. Seward were indifferently doubtful. My objection to the Chiriqui project, and to the impolicy and illegality of Mr. Smith's programme, caused a temporary suspension of the scheme, without any abandonment by the President of his policy of relieving the country of the African race.

In the mean time Congress, responding to the President's views, made appropriations, and one or two projects of colonization in Central America or the West Indies were instituted, Samuel C. Pomeroy, a Senator from Kansas, where he had figured largely in the free State cause, and against the introduction of slavery into that territory, during the Pierce and Buchanan administrations, became interested, and proposed to take upon himself personally an examination of the Central American purchase. An association in New York was also to make an experimental trial by enlisting and carrying out a colony of negroes to the West Indies. The Government was, of course, to furnish a vessel, and be at the expense of what was claimed to be so humane an undertaking. Application was made to the Navy Department for a ship, in order that the colonization fund might be husbanded and spared the expense of chartering a vessel to transport the little colony. This was respectfully declined. The Secretary of the Navy did not feel himself authorized to divert a national ship from its duties for such an object. He had not made estimates for, nor was there an appropriation placed at his disposal for colonization. Recruits went by a different course to Cow Island, a desolate and forlorn place, where a colony was literally planted. Few survived to return. The funds and most of the negroes disappeared together.

President Lincoln, though disappointed in these experiments, by no means abandoned his policy of deportation and emancipation, for the two were in his mind indispensably and indissolubly connected. Colonization in fact had precedence with him. At the beginning of his administration he had brought it forward, and in his first annual message recommended that "steps be taken for colonizing both classes (the free blacks and the slaves that might be emancipated) at some place or places in a climate congenial to them."

In Cabinet meetings, where the subject was frequently discussed, and at the time the preliminary emancipation proclamation was issued, he wished it distinctly understood that deportation was in his mind inseparably connected with that measure; that he considered the two to be parts of one system, and that they must be carried forward together. The preliminary emancipation proclamation was finally decided and promulgated on Monday, the 22d of September, 1862. The subject was discussed and consumed most of the day. The second branch, that of deportation, was postponed to the following meeting on Tuesday, when it was taken up, examined, and debated in all its aspects, without coming to a conclusion, as was also the case on Friday, the 26th, when it was again considered. There was not a member of the Cabinet who did not coincide with the President as to the desirableness of relieving the country of a conflict or of an amalgamation of the two races, one or both of which results lay in the future were they to occupy the same territory. There was, however, great diversity of opinion as to the way and manner of effecting that relief, and also as to its practicability. Although an anti-slavery man, the President was not a convert to the doctrine of the social and political equality of the races, which was a favorite theme of both Sumner and Stevens, with each of whom he had many interviews, and from both of whom he on this point totally differed. Sumner was theoretically and Stevens practically favorable to the social and political equality of blacks and whites. The President doubted if the Africans as a race were themselves capable of organizing as a community and successfully maintaining a government without supervision, or individually susceptible of high intellectual cultivation. There might be and were exceptional cases, but they were by nature dull, inert, dependent, and of little foresight—an ignorant and inferior race, who needed to be governed, were not as a class able or qualified to participate intelligently in self-government. If they were to exercise the high privilege of suffrage—the first

and most important step in free government—it must be at some
distant day in the future after several generations of education
and nurture. In the mean time they would increase in numbers,
have leaders of their own or of a mixed race of exceptionable
ability and ambition, and also white demagogues to excite and
mislead them, until, if they remained with us, a war more
terrible than that in which we were now engaged might be
expected. It was the duty of all who were entrusted with public
affairs to take the subject into consideration, and foresee and
guard against these threatened but he thought certainly impending evils. Colonization he believed to be the only remedy.
His own speeches and writings disclose his sentiments, which are
much misrepresented and misunderstood. He was not a political
Abolitionist. To a deputation of colored persons who waited
upon him said: "You and we are different races. We have a
broader difference than exists between almost any two races."
"Your race suffers very greatly, many of them by living among
us, while ours suffers from your presence. In a word, we suffer
on each side. If this is admitted, it affords a reason at least
why we should be separated. . . . Your race are suffering, in my
judgment, the greatest wrong inflicted on any people. But
even when you cease to be slaves, you are yet far removed from
being placed on an equality with the white race." "Not a single
man of your race is made the equal of a single man of ours."
"It is better for us both, therefore, to be separated."

These extracts indicate the purpose, policy, and kindly
nature of the President, and when, impelled by events, he
decreed emancipation, he connected with it colonization an as
essential part of his policy. But some locality more inviting and
less remote than Liberia he deemed advisable; and encouraged
by the Secretary of the Interior, he still continued to regard with
favor a settlement in Costa Rica. The whole subject was seriously
and earnestly canvassed in successive Cabinet meetings following
the preliminary emancipation in the fall of 1862. Mr. Blair was
a decided advocate of the President's policy; Mr. Bates was
equally so, and going beyond others, he was for compulsory
deportation—compelling the slaves when set free to leave the
country. At one of the meetings he read a carefully prepared

paper expressive of his views. The President was opposed to
compulsory deportation, but would make emigration desirable
and inviting to the blacks. Mr. Seward was indifferently favorable to the President's views, and at his request consulted
with the representatives of foreign governments as to the reception of such a colony. Mr. Chase took no decisive stand in the
Cabinet. I, while assenting to the deleterious effects of the
presence of the colored race, asked how our prosperity would
be affected by sending so much labor out of the country,
even if practicable, doubted the practicability of the scheme,
questioned the validity of the Thompson Chiriqui grant, which
I had inquired into in the spring of 1861, suggested that the
title to the grant itself was defective if not illegal, and questioned whether it was not a positive swindle. Mr. Stanton took
little interest and no active part, but concurred with me on
every point. Mr. Smith excepted to my remarks; said the title
was good beyond question. It had been fully investigated by the
Buchanan administration, which had sent out the expedition
under Commodore Engle to examine the harbor and territory;
he had himself looked into the subject, and knew the men concerned in it to be honorable. The President was surprised and
Blair startled by my doubts of the validity of Thompson's title.
Further action and discussion of the Chiriqui grant was suspended, and Mr. Seward was directed to make inquiries of the
minister from New Granada in regard to the title of Thompson,
and report at a future meeting. In a day or two thereafter Mr.
Seward said he had made inquiries as directed, and that the
governments and rival parties in Central America denied the
validity of the Thompson grant, and pronounced it a bogus
transaction. This terminated all negotiation and inquiry in that
direction, though it did not immediately close the interest and
purpose of the President, who in his second annual message,
alluding to "the future of the free people," said, "I strongly
favor colonization." But it was one of the important measures
of President Lincoln which failed of success—a part of his policy
on which his Cabinet was divided, and in which I for one did
not fully concur, from a conviction of the impracticability of
general deportation, or sending from the country millions of

its inhabitants; not that I adopted the scheme of social and political equality of the races, which was a *sine qua non* with the radicals. Little comparatively has been said on this colonization and deportation policy in which the President took so deep an interest, and in commenting on it he lamented that every humane undertaking of the Government was at once seized by a swarm of swindlers and converted into a mercenary transaction.

Being a constitutionalist, and planting himself on the fundamental principles of the government compromise in the organic law, President Lincoln was reluctant on any occasion or for any purpose, even under the war necessities, to depart from constitutional landmarks. Always cautious, and habitually but inquiringly reticent on controverted and unsettled questions, he moved with deliberation on important subjects, and on no one with greater hesitation than that of emancipating the slaves in the seceding States. It is not surprising, perhaps, that the emotional and more impetuous, but not always the most considerate of his supporters were dissatisfied, and some of them not gentle in their complaints. His own firm purpose in that trying period on the most trying question he had yet encountered will be best understood from his letters and remarks openly and boldly avowed when compelled, or he deemed it expedient to give utterance to his views. His brief reply to a long and intrusively advisory letter of Horace Greeley, written and published by Greeley as "The Prayer of Twenty Millions," discloses the views, object, and intention of Mr. Lincoln. Waiving "the impatient and dictatorial tone" of Greeley, the President said: "As to the policy I seem to be pursuing, as you say, I have not meant to leave any one in doubt. I *would save the* Union. I would save it in the shortest way under the Constitution. The sooner the national authority can be restored, the nearer the Union will be the Union as it was. If there be those who would not save the Union unless they could at the same time save slavery, I do not agree with them. If there be those who would not save the Union unless they could at the same time destroy slavery, I do not agree with them. My paramount object is to save the Union, and not *either* to save or destroy slavery. If I could save the Union without freeing any slaves,

I would do it; if I could save it by freeing all the slaves, I would do it; and if I could do it by freeing some and leaving others alone, I would do that. What I do about slavery and the colored race I do because I believe it helps to save the Union, and what I forbear I forbear because I do not believe it would help to save the Union."

In that extract the aim and policy of the President are seen and explicitly stated. He did not deem it necessary, however, or even expedient, to inform Mr. Greeley and the "twenty millions" for whom Greeley assumed to be the prayerful organ, that he had at that time already prepared and in his desk awaiting events a preliminary proclamation to emancipate the slaves in the seceding States. Others, and many of them, as well as Mr. Greeley, volunteered their opinions and advice as to how the Government should be administered, and admonished the President as to what were his duties. In these cases he listened amid his many duties to what was said, heard suggestions, advice spoken sometimes with friendly regard, sometimes dictatorially uttered, but acted upon his own convictions. The good intentions and abilities of Mr. Greeley he respected, but had not implicit confidence in the judgment and stability of that eminent controversial and philanthropic writer on measures of public policy. Mr. Greeley was at the head of one of the most important and influential political journals of the period, a vigorous and generally lucid writer, with a kindly heart and generous impulses, but he possessed a nasty and irritable temper, was impatient of restraint, and vexed with what he considered the dilatory movements of the Administration in its political proceedings, as well as with the military action of the generals. Benevolently disposed, especially with friends, he was the enemy of slavery and all oppression. As credulous as benevolent, and with no great reverence for settled political principles or fixed ideas of government, he readily listened to new and visionary schemes, was often deceived by inferior intellects that addressed his vanity, was the victim of theories, and of enthusiasts, who enlisted his curiosity, as well as by the cunning and designing, who imposed upon his sympathies and his party prejudices, which were strong. Liberal and tolerant in many things, he was nevertheless imperious and exacting in other and often fanciful schemes, and was seldom satisfied with the management of public affairs, whether by friends or opponents, from a belief that he would in their position do differently and better. His trenchant pen he wielded with power, and often with effect. As the recognized head of one of the first journals he held a commanding position; but not contented in his proper sphere and vocation, he had an insatiable thirst for office, with a conviction that he better than any one could control public opinion and direct the Government. He also flattered himself that he was something of an orator, and that he was as capable and effective a speaker as writer. But with all his talents, he was eminently unfit for administrative duties or responsible office of any kind—was too arbitrary and opinionated to be advised, too erratic, visionary, and impulsive to secure confidence and establish and maintain a consistent line of policy. As an orator, public speaker, or captivating debator in a deliberate body, or even to a miscellaneous gathering, he was unattractive having neither the elocution, grace, magnetic power, fervor, voice, or manner to sway an audience, although he could prepare an interesting essay on almost any subject to be read in a lecture room. But while charitable by nature, and readily dismissing resentments, he never recovered from the humiliation and disappointment which he experienced when made aware that Seward and Weed, the controlling minds of the Whig party in New York, considered him not one of themselves, but only a trusted, secondary, useful, and valuable subordinate to assist and carry out their schemes and purposes. In the peculiar party management of the Whigs in New York in the latter days of the Democratic regency and during Seward's gubernatorial career, the two master spirits exhibited great address in conciliating, uniting, and concentrating others whom they found it convenient to consult, but no third person was incorporated into that dual management. They justly appreciated the abilities of Greeley and valued his services, but they also knew some of his infirmities—his dogmatism by fits; his contempt of certain practices which were to them indispensable; his erratic, unreliable nature in emergencies when his aid was

most wanted—but they did not then fully understand or appreciate his great greed for office, and they were well aware
that his temperament was such that he would be likely in any
responsible public station to bring trouble to his friends and
associates. When the men came to fully understand each other,
and Greeley learned that he was not, as he supposed, one of
three, but only the trusted instrument of two whom he had supposed were his companions and equals, a separation and
alienation took place. They all subsequently acted with the
same party, but the familiarity and intimacy that had been
broken was never restored. Greeley took a step in advance
of his late friends in the Republican movement, left the Whig
organization, which became demoralized, but the remnant of
which continued to be upheld and was under the control of the
two men with whom he had acted, and who were reluctant to
give up an organization that they had controlled with effect
and by which they had sometimes achieved success. In the new
departure Greeley did not conceal his dislike of his two old
associates, was open in his hostility to the nomination of Mr.
Seward for President which Weed had profoundly at heart, and
he was also opposed to Seward's receiving a place in Mr.
Lincoln's Cabinet. The appointment of Seward to the office
of Secretary of State made Greeley less cordial and earnest in
the measures of administration and the support of the policy
pursued. Without his being aware of the fact, he was more
ready to dissent from and to complain of what was done or
omitted to be done than would have been the case had Mr.
Seward not been a conspicuous member of the Government.

Mr. Lincoln was always an anti-slavery man; but, as I have
said, was never a political Abolitionist. Events and war necessity
compelled him to adopt the policy of emancipation, for which
he has received and deserved merited honors; but those who
applaud his course in that respect omit to mention that colonization and deportation of the slaves when set free was deemed
by him an essential part of his emancipation policy. Whether
right or wrong on that subject it is not necessary to discuss, but
the truth need not be suppressed. He believed it would be
best for both the whites and blacks that the latter should leave

the country, or, as he expressed it in his interview with the colored representatives, "it is better for us both to be separated." Knowing his convictions and earnest solicitude on this branch of his policy, I have sometimes doubted whether he would not have hesitated longer in issuing the degree of emancipation had he been aware that colonization would not be accepted as an accompaniment. It is possible at this day for those who were not participants to conceive the perplexities attending the disposition of the slavery question in its various and complex phases, among contending factions and in distinct localities—the differing views in regard to emancipation by men and sections, States and parties, throughout the war. After a year's conflict, and the first step had been taken, and it was evident that slavery was doomed and that freedom to man was to be the future of the country, efforts were made to postpone the day of general deliverance. In the border States the subject of immediate and prospective emancipation was agitated, as in Missouri, and the question was raised whether if one or more of the insurrectionary States, North Carolina for instance, and perhaps others, were to cease hostilities and return to their allegiance to the Constitution and the Union, they could resume their *ante bellum* position, with their laws and institutions unchanged, as members of the Federal Government, having equal political rights with the other States. The people as well as Congress were for a time confused and uncertain on these matters, and discontented friends as well as the opponents of the Administration availed themselves of the occasion and the doubts to declare that the policy of the Executive extinguished all hope of reconciliation, and ensured the everlasting separation of the States.

Questions as to the future of the States that were in rebellion, how they should be recognized or treated when the insurrection was suppressed, and in what way and manner a restoration of their former relation to the Federal Government should be effected, were much agitated in 1863, not only by the considerate and patriotic, but they entered into the schemes of politicians who had personal aspirations and party objects to accomplish. The circumstances of the country indeed required of the

Administration, while prosecuting the war and amid other pressing and absorbing duties, a defined governmental policy for the reëstablishment of the Union. It was a subject of constant thought and of many Cabinet discussions, which eventuated in the adoption of a line of policy that was embodied in the annual message of December 8, 1863, and a proclamation of pardon and amnesty of the same date to all but certain specified persons, with restoration of rights of property, except as to slaves, whenever a prescribed oath was taken of fidelity to the Constitution of the United States, and acquiescence in measures which were the results of the war.

Opposed with the responsibilities which the insurrection and waste of war had brought upon the Government and country, and the strain already made upon the Constitution, the President felt that other and not less weighty measures, affecting the future and permanent welfare of the country, were pressing upon him, impelling him to predicate a course by which the suspended or broken relations of the family of States could again be restored and nationalized. This matter of reconstruction, rehabilitating the States in insurrection after the rebellion had been suppressed, was indeed the great, overpowering, and most important work of the Administration. On it depended the enduring peace and welfare of the States, the happiness and prosperity of the people, and the stability and perpetuity of the Union itself. In the disposition of the subject bitter contentions arose, which, if partially allayed, were not fully adjusted under the administration of Mr. Lincoln, and after his death increased in intensity, changed in some respects the character of the Government, and entering into party conflicts, caused political alienations which disturbed the local and national elections that have not yet terminated, and may outlast the republic. The wild, revolutionary, and destructive schemes of some of his most prominent supporters, who were determined to centralize and consolidate the Government and reduce the States to the condition of provinces, found no favor with President Lincoln. On the other hand, the factious Democratic opposition, which interposed obstruction to almost every important and necessary measure, and which seldom in that

trying period rose above the lowest level of party, excepted to
the exercise of extraordinary Executive authority, though essential to the salvation of the Union. The President, neither
impelled by the one nor restrained by the other of these extremes, and surrounded by a multitude of threatening difficulties, continued cool, calm and resolutely deliberate, but cou-
rageously firm in his reconstruction policy when action became
necessary. Slow and reluctant to adopt emancipation, fully
aware that in peaceful times the institution of slavery was
protected by constitutional restrictions and safeguards, he had
been unwilling to touch it, even under war necessity, but the
exigency required governmental action. In his message of December, 1863, he said: "According to our political system, as
a matter of civil administration, the Government had no lawful power to effect emancipation in any State, and for a long
time it had been hoped that the rebellion could be suppressed
without resorting to it as a military measure. It was all the
while deemed possible that the necessity for it might come,
and that if it should, the crisis for the contest would then be
presented. It came, and as was anticipated, was followed by
dark and doubtful days."

In this extract the feelings and ideas of the President in
that first cautious but necessary step are frankly stated. It was
not a voluntary movement on his part, but slavery lay at the
basis of national strife, and after war commenced emancipation was indispensable to unity and the national welfare. A
year later, but while the war was still in progress, and the
rebels, though weakened, were still vigorous and in arms, the
conviction that the Union cause would triumph was general,
and the question of the future of the Government and country,
and how the States were to be reconstructed, and in their federal relations brought into harmonious action, was discussed.
There was no wish with certain parties for a restoration of
the old Union. The radicals preferred a consolidated central
government, with supervisory authority over the States, to a
federal Union, with reserved local sovereignty and an equality
of political rights among the several commonwealths. The
President recognized and admitted the necessity of indicating

the policy of the Administration, but to the disappointment and chagrin of many friends, his policy was still one of reconciliation and a federal Union, with as little disturbance as possible of the governments and traditions of the rebel States, and a sacred regard of the constitutional rights of the erring as well as of the unfortunate. He said in his message in 1863: "Looking now to the present and future, and with a reference to a resumption of the national authority in the States wherein that authority has been suspended, I have thought fit to issue a proclamation in which 'nothing is attempted beyond what is amply justified by the Constitution.' " The suggestion in the proclamation as to maintaining the political framework of the States on what is called reconstruction is made in the hope it may do good, without danger of harm." "This question is beset with the conflicting views that the step might be delayed too long or taken too soon."

As a basis of action for the loyally disposed citizens of any State to effect reconciliation and promote reconstruction or a restoration of the States to their former rightful position in the Federal Union, he declared that any "number of persons not less than one-tenth in number of the votes cast in such State at the Presidential election of the year of our Lord one thousand eight hundred and sixty, each having taken the oath aforesaid, and not having since violated it, and *being a qualified voter by the election law of the State existing before the so-called act of secession,* AND EXCLUDING ALL OTHERS, shall reëstablish a State government which shall be republican, and in no wise contravening said oath, such *shall be recognized as the true government of the State,* and the State shall receive thereunder the benefits of the constitutional provision which declares that 'the United States shall guarantee to every State in this Union a republican form of government, and shall protect each of them against invasion, and on application of the Legislature, or the Executive, when the Legislature cannot be convened, against domestic violence.' And it is suggested as not improper that in constructing a legal State government in any State, the name of the State, the boundary, the subdivisions, the Constitution, and the general code of laws as before the rebellion be maintained, etc. . . . This proclamation is intended to present the people of the States wherein the *national authority has been suspended* and legal State governments have been subverted, a mode in and by which the national authority and legal State governments may be reëstablished within said States or any portion of them."

President Lincoln's plan to reëstablish a State government in any of the seceding States was plain and simple. The mode of reconstruction was fully discussed and concurred in by every member of his Cabinet. It was said there were members of Congress who would dissent from this action of the Executive, and there was some question in regard to the number of voters which on the first attempt should initiate reorganization. One-tenth was agreed upon. On no one point were the members of the Administration more united than that of designating what persons should vote and participate in the election. In the several States different and peculiar qualifications of suffrage were established, the subject having been reserved when the Constitution was framed for the local governments. It being an ungranted power, no uniform national regulation could be ordered, nor was it desirable that there should be if State individuality was to be considered. Each commonwealth had best determined that question in other and peaceful days, when they knew and had deliberately enacted for themselves who should be entrusted, with the elective franchise and what was best for their own self government. But it was proper for the President to withhold pardon, and thereby exclude from voting, the primary source of government, and from participation in civil affairs, at least for a period and until order and peace were established, rebels in arms who had forfeited citizenship and life by resisting the Government and putting the laws at defiance. These had forfeited the voting privilege, and in fact all their civil rights; but the President, in the exercise of his prerogative, extended pardon and general amnesty to such as laid down their arms, returned to their allegiance, and complied with the conditions prescribed for restoration and union. Besides excluding those who were in open rebellion, it was important that strangers—persons belonging to the armies and not legal residents, but who were brought thither by the war—

should be precluded. The idea that the Administration or Federal Government was authorized to admit any to vote who were not legally qualified and entitled by the laws of the State in which they were temporarily located to do so, was not entertained or even suggested. No one proposed or believed that negroes or colored persons, even those who had intelligence or property, but were not permitted the elective franchise by the organic law of the States, should or could be endowed with the privilege of voting by the President or Congress. The Federal Government was clothed with no power to enlarge suffrage, but the President could circumscribe it by withholding or by conditional pardons could remove forfeitures and grant amnesty to the inhabitants, which he did by his proclamation. Suffrage was withheld from actual rebels; but there was no attempt to enlarge, extend, or change the local law of suffrage of any State.

The purpose to abstain as far as possible from federal interference in the State governments was by no means satisfactory to the radicals. The leaders and many of their less intelligent followers had in view the subversion and even the annihilation of the State governments, an avowed purpose to territorialize the States which had attempted to secede, and reduce them to the condition of provinces, to subjugate the people and govern them, instead of permitting the people to govern themselves, and to no longer recognize State equality. It was in fact an innovation on, if not the immediate destruction of our federal republican system—a change, revolutionary in its character, to be brought by a fragmentary Congress, in the name of freedom, humanity, and equal rights. Connected with this ultra scheme and ultimately a part of the radical plan was a design, openly declared, not only to disfranchise most of the intelligent whites, but of conferring on every negro the privilege of voting. Senator Sumner, the champion leader of this revolutionary project, and others claimed that suffrage was not a privilege, but an innate right to which colored persons were entitled, if not by the Constitution, by the Declaration of Independence, which recognized all men as equals, and that it was the duty of the Federal Government to secure to them its exercise, regardless of local govern-

ments and the reserved powers and sovereignty of the States.
In private caucusses and conversations it was urged that the
negro vote was right in itself and that it would secure permanent
ascendancy to the Republican party. But the appeals and the
current party opinion failed to influence President Lincoln,
who considered the proposition to disregard the fundamental
laws and reserved rights of the States as an outrage that would
ultimately be ruinous in its consequences to our federal system.
Nor was there a single member of the Cabinet who gave con-
tinuous countenance to the project of forcing negro suffrage
upon the States. On the contrary, it was the policy of the
President, distinctly and unequivocally declared and always
consistently maintained, that only qualified voters by the election "laws of the State existing immediately before the so-called
act of secession," should vote on the question of reëstablishing
a State government, or, in common parlance, reconstruction.
There was diversity, it may be said contrariety of opinions in
the Cabinet on incidental and minor points connected with the
subject of reconstruction, such as emancipation, colonization,
confiscation, amnesty, and acts of Executive authority without
Congressional action to reorganize and rehabilitate the States
in insurrection, but there was perfect agreement by the President
and Cabinet on the subject of non-interference by the Federal
Government with the laws of the States on the question of
suffrage. At a later period two members of the Cabinet, Chase
and Stanton, advocated the establishment and enforcement of
negro suffrage in the rebel States, the former as a political right,
the latter as a measure of expediency, but neither of these gentlemen proposed or suggested it in the autumn of 1863, when
the policy of reconstruction was discussed.

Mr. Chase, always an anti-slavery man, was a favorite and
recognized leader of that class of persons. With great ambition
and high political aspirations, he was covetous of his position
as a chief in the anti-slavery cause, but sensitive on the subject
of being considered a political Abolitionist, always disclaiming
connection with that organization. The war and the exercise
of strong measures by the Government had rendered that faction
and their unconstitutional schemes less obnoxious than in for-

mer years. No member of the Administration was more surprised than the Secretary of the Treasury when the President
in the autumn of 1862 announced to the Cabinet his purpose
to issue a proclamation to emancipate slaves in the rebel States.
Until made known by himself in full Cabinet meeting, I am not
aware that any member of the Administration but Mr. Seward
and myself (one a Whig, the other a Democrat, in their political
antecedents) had been advised that he had the subject in con-
templation. I have some reason to suppose that Owen Lovejoy,
the avowed and leading Abolitionist in Congress, was confi-
dentially consulted. Neither the Secretary of the Treasury nor
the Postmaster General was present when the proclamation was
first submitted to the other members of the Cabinet. When
first submitted to the full Cabinet the President declared the
act to be his own, for which no member of his Administration
was responsible. It came upon Mr. Chase, as he stated, unexpectedly, but he cordially approved the measure. The step was,
however, beset with many perplexing and embarrassing difficulties to the Administration. Universal emancipation throughout the republic was not decreed by the President, as many in
these days suppose. The measure did not reach the border States,
nor was it nor could it be extended over any State that had not
rebelled. To have attempted it would have been an unauthorized
assumption of power, warranted by no military necessity, nor
could the Executive by any act of his or the Administration
forbid the reëstablishment of slavery or the enactment of laws
respecting labor or servitude in any State after the rebellion was
suppressed. As against foreign powers the rights of an American
citizen were maintained by the Federal Government, but the
local organizations were his protection in the United States.
What, it was asked, would be the condition of any one of the
seceding States should her people voluntarily abandon the Confederacy and now come forward to resume federal allegiance
and fidelity to the Union? Would her position as one of the
United States be like that of New York and Massachusetts?
There had been a disposition manifested and some progress
made in North Carolina toward reunion under the flag, and
efforts were still being made to detach one or more of the

seceding States from the Confederacy, and effect its complete restoration to the political family independent of its associates. Were North Carolina to cease hostilites and come forward under the proclamation to resume her place, would she also resume all her original sovereign rights as before the rebellion? Would she be in the political condition of Maryland and other border States? Would her slave owners retain their slaves under North Carolina laws? Would the State have exclusive control of the subject and the same sovereign rights as before the rebellion? And if not, if deprived of a sovereign right never ceded to the central Government, but specially reserved by the federal Constitution, she would not be on an equal footing with the other States. If dispossessed of this or any other right which was enjoyed by her co-States, what inducement was there for her to reunite? The original constitutional compact would be destroyed; the States would be no longer equal in political rights, as had been agreed when the Constitution was framed. A primary fundamental axiom of our federal system would be arbitrarily set aside by the central Government. Indeed, it was claimed that emancipation had destroyed that equality, and that the border States had privileges of which other States south of them were deprived. Where under the Constitution had the Federal Government authority to make these discriminations or distinctions?

While the other members of the Administration felt the embarrassment of these complications, and no one more than the President, Mr. Chase, who had been startled by the unexpected action in the proclamation of freedom, pressed forward, breaking over all barriers, and entertained, or professed to entertain, no doubt in regard to the present or the future. Emancipation, though by an Executive order issued upon military necessity, had effected, he claimed, a permanent change in the federal Constitution. Liberty was, by rebellion and the decision of arms, to which appeal had by the rebels themselves been made, become a part of the organic law of the republic, and freedom was hereafter the national birthright of every citizen. When it was denied that a change in the Constitution could be made by an Executive proclamation, Mr. Chase, a Statist and not a centralist, insisted that the change had already taken place. The fact that slavery was recognized and still existed in the border States he accounted as nothing—as hardly a temporary obstruction, a frail remnant, which would be swept away by the mighty wave of public opinion probably before the rebellion was suppressed. In this decisive stand and these emphatic declarations of the Secretary of the Treasury, conflicting as they did with his political doctrines as a Statist, it was surmised that other ends than those of slavery and emancipation might be found; that the President having by his emancipation policy taken a step in advance of the Cabinet officer who was considered the prominent anti-slavery champion in the Administration, that gentleman was determined not to surrender his position, but thenceforward to be in the fore-front rank on all these questions. It is undoubtedly true that the President in coming to the conclusion of emancipating the slaves in the rebel States had done so without first consulting the Secretary of the Treasury, or advising with him until after the preliminary proclamation was written, and in doing so he doubtless had a purpose. It is no less true that Mr. Chase detected and comprehended that purpose; but, though unadvised of the measure at its inception, he was unflinching in its support when it was announced, and thenceforward steadfastly and persistently insisted on its rigid enforcement by the Executive, with all its embarrassments and responsibilities. This was, however, with professed deference and friendly regard toward the President, who, he had a lingering hope, but with serious doubts, was not to be a candidate for reëlection, and with whom he desired to act in concert on matters concerning which he was well aware there were differences in the Cabinet and the Republican party.

Reconstruction, or the method of rehabilitating the States, reëstablishing the Federal Government in its rightful authority and securing permanent union throughout the limits of the republic, were questions discussed and agitated in the autumn of 1863, and politicians connected them with the approaching Presidential election. The plan communicated in the annual message at the opening of the session in December was an Executive measure, suggesting what was deemed a practicable policy tending to reconstruction, which had been deliberately considered in the Cabinet and unanimously approved by every member of the Administration.

Speculations in regard to the ensuing Presidential election had commenced among the politicians and party men, and although the subject was never alluded to in the Cabinet, the probable candidates of the Republican party were not inattentive to current public opinion. There was a growing impression among the Republicans that the President would not and ought not to decline a reëlection; that his continuance in office was essential until the rebellion was suppressed; and that under his guidance and management the union and tranquility of the country could be best accomplished. Mr. Seward, aware that he had lost confidence and possessed less strength than in 1860, when he failed of a nomination, came early to the conclusion that he would not be a competitor with Mr. Lincoln; but he still had a corps of efficient friends who, like himself, were determined that no other man should supersede him, and especially not his former rival and present associate in the Cabinet, Mr. Chase. But the Secretary of the Treasury, though not in his proper sphere in the Treasury, nor particularly successful as a financier, had from his official position and extreme official patronage, and his early and continued antislavery opinions, acquired strength and a considerable personal following. His mental and physical powers were great, and were actively employed in discharging duties for which he had little taste, but he was never forgetful that he might be useful in a higher place. Not very skilful in political tactics, or correct in his estimate of men, and often deceived by those who had a purpose to accomplish in deceiving him, he lost favor in one quarter while he gained in another. With lingering hopes, but serious doubts whether the President would or would not be a candidate for reëlection, and unwilling, but nevertheless prepared, if public opinion would sustain him, to compete for the nomination, he, during the autumn of 1863 and early months to 1864, exerted himself to gain the good will and support of the Republicans, and particularly the radical portion of that party.

6

Administration of Abraham Lincoln, IV

RADICAL PLOTTINGS AGAINST MR. LINCOLN

The election of 1864 brought into the open many of the
issues dividing radicals and conservatives. So formidable
did the opposition to Lincoln become that even members
of the Cabinet lent themselves to the designs of the
President's opponents. In this essay, the Secretary of the
Navy describes how Lincoln convinced both party and
country not to "swap horses in midstream."

THE PATRIOTIC MEN of all parties in the free States
responded with alacrity to the calls of the Executive for assistance and support during the civil war. There was an element—a remnant of the broken Democratic organization—which
throughout the entire struggle persistently opposed every measure of the Government to sustain the Union and the flag. Scarcely less annoying and embarrassing to the Administration, though
not as fully and generally understood, were the factious and
discontented intrigues which existed in the Republican party.
That party was composed of individuals who had not been
homogeneous in their political principles or party action prior
to the interposition of the federal Government in the affairs
of Kansas, but who, irrespective of old party organizations,
united to vindicate the right of the people to frame their own
government. After the election of Mr. Lincoln, on which they
agreed, and to elect whom they put forth their combined
strength, the discordant materials of the newly created party
began to manifest differences, and although all united in prose-

The Galaxy, XXIV (November, 1877).

123

cuting the war, there was disagreement as to the method of conducting it, and soon as to the results to be obtained. The members of Congress were not all statesmen, or even intelligent politicians, but nearly all were violent partisans. The policy of the President was generally acceptable to the considerable and rightly disposed of his supporters, but did not give satisfaction to either extreme in Congress. Failing to dictate to or control him, exception was taken to his measures, especially to his amnesty proclamation, and, assuming that the legislative branch of the Government was supreme and absolute, his course was opposed, and a counteracting policy was projected by the radicals.

A scheme or plan for what was called reconstruction had been contrived and adroitly prepared, during the first session of the Thirty-eighth Congress, by certain radicals in Congress, under the leadership of Henry Winter Davis, a talented representative of Maryland, acute, but not always politic, and of centralizing tendencies, the main object of which was to counteract the mild and tolerant policy of the Administration; to deny to the States in insurrection representation; to prevent reunion with the express assent of Congress; and to compel the construction of new constitutions by or for the States in rebellion, which should embrace certain doctrinal points indicated in a proposed law, which Congress had no rightful authority to enact. This revolutionary and mischievously designed enactment, initiated by Davis in December, 1863, was reported by a select committee, of which Davis was chairman, pending the election and assembling of delegates to the Republican national convention, which convened at Baltimore on the 7th of June, 1864. It was held for some time in abeyance, to influence party action, but passed the House of Representatives on the 4th of May by a vote of 74 in the affirmative, all of whom were Republicans, and 66 in the negative, all but six of whom were Democrats. A vicious partisan preamble, prepared by Davis himself, and reported by the committee, was stricken out in the House by a majority of eighteen; more than twenty Republicans voting against it, most of them dissenting from the radical opposition to the Executive.

In the Senate, Mr. Wade of Ohio, chairman of the Committee on Territories, who acted in concert with Davis, reported the bill, with two slight amendments, on the 27th of May, ten days before the meeting of the national nominating convention of the Republicans. It finally passed, six Republicans and every Democrat voting against it, and was submitted to President Lincoln just as Congress was about to adjourn, when there was no time to prepare a veto; nor could the radical test movement to cramp the Executive by encroaching upon his prerogative, and limiting his constitutional rights, have been suppressed without endangering the unity of the Republican organization, and perhaps entirely breaking down the Administration majority in Congress.

President Lincoln beheld with regret these intrigues, but, earnestly and sincerely desirous for the speedy restoration of peace and national unity, he could not, with his conviction of duty, have given his approval to the project of Davis and his radical associates, which was destructive of our federal system. Under the many difficulties and embarrassments which beset the Administration, growing out of the civil war, extraordinary powers had, as already stated, been necessarily exercised by the Government. The President, oppressed with responsibility, had lamented this necessity; but its exercise by the Executive engendered in the irresponsible majority of Congress—for responsibility there was divided among two hundred—a wild and latitudinous spirit, until the radicals assumed for the legislative branch of the Government omnipotent and unlimited powers above and beyond the other departments of the Government and of the Constitution itself. Not content with the discharge of their legislative functions, they assumed under the war powers executive and judicial authority, and when the rebellion drew to a close arrogated the right of reducing States to a territorial, dependent condition, and of altering and dictating to them their form and framework of government, and of making for them in fact new constitutions. This was the policy of Stevens, Davis, Wade, and the radicals generally, as well as of Sumner, who did not always fellowship with the others; but it was not the policy of Mr. Lincoln. Always disinclined to controversy, he was extremely reluctant at this peculiar period to have, in addition to his other labors and difficulties, a conflict with the radical extremists, who claimed that they they were better Republicans than himself; that the legislative branch was the Government; that the other departments were subordinate; that the Executive must devise no policy, must do no act nor take any step toward restoration, reorganization, reconstruction of the Union, or recognition of the States, without first receiving the permission and assent of Congress.

The radicals assumed that the Union was broken, and, dissatisfied with the tolerant and conservative intentions of the President, were determined to make issue with him as to the manner of conducting the war, and of reëstablishing the general Government. The immense armies, indifferently commanded, the meager results, and the waste and expense of the brief summer campaigns of 1864, were exhausting the enthusiasm and patience of the people.

The radical scheme of reconstruction was artfully contrived to turn the national discontent consequent on the failure of the generals against the President, and many ardent and impulsive minds, in the excitement of party and the uneasiness of the times, were deluded and deceived. Under the pretext of the clause in the Constitution which declares "the United States shall guarantee to every State in this Union a republican form of government," it was claimed that Congress could dictate to the States which had been in rebellion their fundamental law, and compel them to abandon their old constitutions and governmental traditions, and the usages which they and their fathers had prescribed, and frame new constitutions, embracing principles and doctrines that were unacceptable, and which had not been in issue in the war. No authority for this exercise of Congressional power was specified, but that of the word "guarantee," to which H. Winter Davis and his associates ascribed a new definition. It was insisted that to guarantee was not to secure to them their own respective governments, adopted by themselves, and under which they had lived prior to 1861, but it was to make, to create, to direct, to control, and impose upon them new constitutions, embracing certain fundamental prin-

ciples of government in regard to suffrage and local self-government, which the States had reserved and never delegated. Thousands and tens of thousands, wishing to subjugate and wreak
vengeance on the secessionists, subscribed to this new definition
or interpretation of the word "guarantee." The essence and
intent of this radical question was to confer the privilege of
voting on ignorant negroes, and to make its exercise by intelligent whites the exception. But Mr. Lincoln was neither deceived
by this extraordinary definition or perversion of the word "guarantee," nor diverted from the path of duty by the specious
pretence and appeals of the radicals; nor was he deterred from
an honest discharge of his obligations to the Constitution, and
a faithful support of the federal and State governments, by the
insinuation that his Republicanism was questionable, nor by
assertions that he was feeble or too lenient toward the rebels,
and not sufficiently energetic in the conduct of the war. He did
not subscribe to the doctrine that the States where slavery existed,
or where negroes were excluded from suffrage, were not republican, nor admit that the "guarantee" prescribed in the Constitution intended the abolition of slavery and the destruction of
existing State governments.

Almost every State, at the time the Union was formed, and
when the Constitution was adopted, authorized slavery. Yet all
were recognized as having a "republican form of government."
Such were the principles and views of the fathers. No one in 1861,
at the commencement of the war, had denied that the governments of Virginia and Missouri, or even those of South Carolina
and Louisiana, were republican. Nor were they less republican
after the slaves were emancipated. They had in all other respects
the same institutions, customs, traditions, and usages in 1864
that they had prior to 1861. The federal Constitution was,
moreover, formed and adopted by the States, acting not only
in the aggregate, but separately, each for itself—all were represented—none were excluded in the national convention of 1787,
when mutual concessions and compromises were made; but it
was proposed in 1864, and subsequently, by the representatives
of a part of the States, to exclude others, and to make and impose
new conditions for the States not permitted to be represented,

to dictate new terms to them, and to establish by legislation a
new constitution of government, which, if insisted on in 1789,
would have defeated any federal government or union of the
States. This was now to be effected by excluding all the States
which had been engaged in rebellion—constituting one-third of
the whole—from representation, or voice, or participation in
the change proposed to be made. The excuse and justification
for this assumption was the novel interpretation of the words
"guarantee" and "republican form of government," which it
was claimed conferred grants of power that had not been exercised during seventy years of our national existence. President
Lincoln would not permit himself to be beguiled, deluded, or
led astray by any such pretence, though demanded by a majority of his nominal supporters in Congress, embracing some
of the most talented and active members of the Republican
party. These uneasy spirits, that could pull down but not build
up, received encouragement from political aspirants, who pan-
dered to their emotional demands.

To suppress the insurrection and the rebellion, reëstablish
the union of all the States, and at the same time observe and
preserve the rights of each and of the federal Government,
were matters of deep and general interest to the people, and
important duties of the Administration. They occupied unceasing attention. Different views were entertained by the political
friends of the President on each of these questions, and there
was the persistent party opposition of that portion of the
Democracy—most of them "peace Democrats"—that combined
against the Government, and deprecated the prosecution of the
war. These peace Democrats, and all who adhered to that organization, were unreasonable if not unpatriotic, and so intensely
partisan that little support or encouragement was expected of
them. It was the friends who opposed his measures and ob-
structed his policy who embarrassed the President and sometimes crippled his action. His Republican opponents were
either fanatics or factious. Many of them had no desire for a
restored or continued federal Union, claiming that war had
dissolved political relations and unsettled the Government. They
were for altering or modifying the Constitution, and in favor

of a change from the federal system of State equality to one of a more central and consolidated character.

Great disappointment was felt by the radical leaders when they became convinced that the President would not yield and identify himself with their revolutionary schemes, and participate in or be a party to their designs. But from the day he was inaugurated the polar star which guided his course was the Constitution, and as essential to its stability was the preservation of the federal Union. The Constitution and the Union were with him, and must ever be with an honest and patriotic President, above and beyond any and all mere party or personal considerations. Compelled to exercise authority which a state of peace would not have justified or permitted, he was bitterly denounced by the peace Democrats at almost every step and for every extraordinary but necessary act. They would not admit that the President was clothed with any authority not expressly conferred, even for the preservation of the national existence against State and sectional organizations for its destruction. On the other hand, his radical friends from the beginning accused him of inefficiency, imbecility, and want of proper energy, because he hesitated to resort to extreme measures and the exercise of any and all authority, however arbitrary, which they deemed expedient. It is easier to criticise actions and measures after events have transpired than it was to strike out the true course to be pursued when chaos prevailed, and Government and people encountered an overwhelming and blinding storm which threatened them with wreck and ruin.

The emergency did not permit of delay, nor yet were rash and inconsiderate measures to be resorted to. National union was to be preserved; State insurrection, though under legal forms, was to be suppressed. The President and those associated with him felt the responsibility in all its delicacy and importance, and every step was taken with cautious deliberation, but with intelligent decision and firmness. The times required a calm, considerate, but firm policy. The condition of the country was without precedent or parallel. No provision of the Constitution met or provided for the crisis. Such an insurrection—organized rebellion by State governments, and resistance by States

and people to the federal authority and laws, carrying with it
the destruction of the general Government, the Union, and the
whole federal system—had never been anticipated by the fathers
of the Constitution. The war had been commenced by the secession leaders with a determination to separate from and break
up the Union. They were met, and the war for more than two
years had been continued under the direction of the President
to maintain the national integrity without infringing on the
reserved rights of the States, accompanied with constant efforts
on his part to harmonize the conflicting elements, restore peace,
and preserve unimpaired both federal and State rights. With
these great ends in view he, on the 8th of December, 1863,
issued the proclamation of amnesty under his constitutional
"power to grant reprieve and pardon for offences against the
United States," and also by authority of an act of Congress
which declares that the President is authorized "by proclamation
to extend to persons who may have participated in the existing
rebellion pardon and amnesty, at such times and on such conditions as he may deem expedient for the public welfare";
granting to "all persons who have, directly or by implication,
participated in the existing rebellion," with certain specified
exceptions, a full pardon to "each of them, with restoration of
all rights of property except as to slaves, on condition they would
take and subscribe an oath, and thenceforward keep and maintain" it. The oath required them to "faithfully support, protect,
and defend the Constitution of the United States and the union
of the States thereunder." The amnesty proclamation, with its
generous and liberal terms to the rebels, and its restrictive
prohibition that none but qualified voters by the election law
of the State should vote in reëstablishing the suspended
State government, met with instant and violent opposition.
On the colored population, who were to be trained by intruding adventurers, the radical managers were relying for
permanent party ascendancy through the South. But these
anticipated recruits were prohibited from voting in the reëstablishment of State governments by the President's policy, which
expressly excluded them.

The amnesty proclamation brought out distinctly the dif-

ference between President Lincoln and the positive or radical element of the Republican party in the winter of 1864.
That difference a few years later eventuated in malevolent hostility to the Administration, and the impeachment
of President Johnson. The great objects of President Lincoln
and his Cabinet were peace, the maintenance of the federal system, and a restoration of the Union with as little disturbance of
the Constitution and the structure of the Government as possible. Were the rebels to disband and quietly resume their position, acquiescing in the changes which the war, brought on
by themselves, had effected in regard to slavery, the proceeding
would have been comfortable to his views, and satisfactory as
an adjustment. Slavery, the cause of the war or the original
pretext for it, had been disposed of by the war itself. Prior to
the rebellion, the institution, as slavery was called, was secured
to the States, and its existence or extinction depended on or
was at the discretion of the States respectively. It was strictly
a reserved municipal State right, specially protected and guaranteed to the States where it existed by the fundamental federal
law. But not content with this constitutional local security, the
slaveholders claimed that slavery was national; that it should
be extended and carried into the Territories, and have new
national guarantees. This not being conceded or admitted,
they strove to break up the Union, and appealed to arms in the
cause of slavery. The issue thus made by themselves became
national, and the permanency of slavery itself entered into the
secession contest by the acts of the slave States.

So long as he could, the President avoided the issue presented. When, however, in the progress of the war, he became
convinced that the slaves were employed against the Government, that they must be against or for us, that the fate of
slavery was doomed, that the alternative of its abolition or the
downfall of the Government was involved and could not be
evaded, he did not hesitate to act. No course was left him but
that of a declaration of emancipation, which he made after
proper warning. This warning was disregarded, and thenceforward the result was inevitable. Every one had become convinced, even before emancipation was pronounced, that in the

suppression of the rebellion slavery, the alleged cause of national strife, would cease to exist throughout the republic. It was never doubted by the administration that the federal Government would be successful in the conflict, and the integrity of the Union maintained.

The year which elapsed after emacipation was first announced demoralized and exhausted the rebels, but another and more advanced step became necessary. The Executive felt it a duty to facilitate, by such means and power as he possessed, the resumption of federal and State authority where it had been suspended, even if but a small minority in each seceding State responded. The idea of embracing the opportunity of a civil war to revolutionize the one or break down the other—a favorite scheme of the radicals—never entered his thoughts, was repugnant to his convictions, and opposed to all his views, principles, and intentions. Reconstruction, restoration, and peace were, however, to be effected in a legal and constitutional way, not, as was urged by the peace Democrats, by negotiations with rebels in arms, not by commissioners between the contending parties as with a foreign power, for that would be a recognition and admission that the rebel organization was legal and national while the people of the States in insurrection were citizens of the United States in revolt, resisting federal laws and defying federal authority. When the rebels should lay down their arms and resume their duties as citizens of the United States, their States would be relieved of the usurped, secession, illegal governments, and each commonwealth would resume its legal, constitutional, and rightful position as a State and member of the federal Union. But how was this work of reconciliation and restoration to begin? The rebels demanded it should be by commissioners appointed by the respective parties, as between belligerents of different powers or nationalities, thereby securing recognition and making the Confederacy legitimate. The peace Democrats took the same position so far as to blame the Administration for not accepting the proposition and appointing commissioners. This matter of negotiation as between two governments had been a point with the rebel leaders from the beginning, before they made an assault on the garrison in Fort Sumter. The object was well understood, but never for a moment was the idea that the insurrection was legal entertained by the President or any member of the Administration. The insurrection was illegal, and to be suppressed by federal law and authority. The time had arrived when it became a duty to act—a time which the President aptly said was not to "be delayed too long or taken too soon." He therefore, with the unanimous approval of the Cabinet, issued his amnesty proclamation extending pardon to all citizens who would return to their duty, and inviting States to resume their true, legal, and legitimate position in the Union. It was intended as an initiative measure in the interests of peace and union, deliberately, considerately, and wisely taken, but it gave great offence to the radical friends of the Administration, who arrayed themselves at once in opposition and contributed to defeat the policy of reëstablishing the Government on the original constitutional basis without still further change than the emancipation policy, and it was insisted that emancipation should not be decreed by the Executive until "after obtaining the assent of Congress."

The opportunity of the Presidential election was seized upon as a means of accomplishing their purpose of discarding Mr. Lincoln and his policy, and also getting rid of his Cabinet. There were, however, differences among the malcontents and aspirants in the Republican party, not only in theory, but as to the candidate upon whom they would concentrate. The prevailing sentiment among them at the beginning favored the nomination of Salmon P. Chase, the Secretary of the Treasury. This gentleman had an ambition to be President, but was extremely cautious and circumspect in committing himself to any movement antagonistic to his chief. Differences had existed between him and the Secretary of State, commencing with and even preceding the formation of Mr. Lincoln's Cabinet, which were never wholly overcome. These differences called into activity the vigilance of Mr. Seward and his friends, who, as well as all his associates in the Cabinet, Mr. Chase became aware, watched every movement, and, he was soon convinced, aided to detect and defeat every scheme to substitute Chase for Lincoln. Although he numbered among his partisans some of the leading and most influential Republicans in Congress, and the Treasury officials were largely in his interest, there were no indications of an extensive feeling for him on the part of the people. In the confident belief that he had a strong hold on the popular mind in New Hampshire, the State of his nativity, and in Ohio, of which he was a citizen, an earnest effort was made in the winter and spring of 1864 to procure from the Republicans in these two States an expression of preference in his favor; but it resulted in a total failure in each State, for in their party conventions the sentiment was overwhelmingly, almost unanimously, for the renomination and reëlection of Mr. Lincoln. As great unanimity was manifested in other States, sufficient to convince men less sanguine than the Secretary of the Treasury that the Republicans as a party desired the continuance of the administration of Mr. Lincoln for another term. He therefore, on the 8th of March, stated in a published letter that he had some time previously said, "Should our friends in Ohio manifest a preference for another, I should accept their decision with the ready acquiescence due," etc.; and the recent action of the Union members indicated such a preference; therefore it became him to withdraw as a candidate. In withdrawing he dwelt on the importance of energy, and the union of efforts to suppress the rebellion, themes urged by his friends, but it was noticed gave no intimation or wish in behalf of the President with whom he was associated, and for whom his constituents had declared their preference with great unanimity.

The malcontents in the Republican party were not inattentive and inactive during the winter, but instituted a secret organization of which Samuel C. Pomeroy, a Senator from Kansas of unfortunate notoriety, was chairman. Pomeroy was an adventurer from Massachusetts, sent into Kansas in the early days of that Territory as the agent of an association in Boston, to aid in resisting the encroachment of slavery and assist in establishing free government. He was reputed to have so managed his agency as to advance his own personal interest quite as much as that of the association in whose behalf he acted, and shortly after Kansas was made a State, succeeded in procuring the election of himself to the United States Senate, where, in the disturbed condition of affairs growing out of the civil war, and the agitation of the slave question, he was recognized for his zeal in the radical cause. Having always his personal and pecuniary interest in view, Pomeroy soon ingratiated himself with the Treasury, and readily consented to take the place of chairman of a committee, self-constituted or privately appointed in this new scheme, which he and his associates were induced to believe would supersede the Republican organization. It was a flank movement against President Lincoln, who was assailed by the Democrats for prosecuting what they denounced as a relentless and ruinous war at the same time that the radicals accused him of lack of energy and of too great forbearance toward the rebels. There was not, however, perfect accord between the radicals and their ambitious but conservative allies or fellow laborers in the Republican party. The former, over confident from their success in controlling Congressional action, were resolute and unyielding against the reëlection of Mr. Lincoln regardless of consequences, while the latter were not prepared to engage in the contest unless well satisfied they could be successful. Mr. Chase was the representative man of such conservatives as were opposed to Mr. Lincoln, and their avowed candidate. The radicals accepted him not from choice, but because he was considered the most available and prominent man for the position, and was avowedly for a more energetic prosecution of the war. Pomeroy was the willing agent of both factions, and agreed with both. Though by no means inclined to go into a minority for any principle, he, after his successful experience in Kansas, persuaded himself that with Treasury patronage the head of that department could be nominated and elected. With these feelings and these backers, a circular was prepared in Washington and issued, to which Pomeroy's name was appended, and which he and his associates extensively circulated for the purpose of initiating, combining, and stimulating the movement for Mr. Chase. This circular so distinctly presents the views and purposes of those engaged in the opposition to Mr. Lincoln, by the radical and discontented Republicans, that it should be read and understood, in order to rightly comprehend the intrigue of that date:

[CONFIDENTIAL]
WASHINGTON, D. C., FEBRUARY, 1864.

Sir: The movements recently made throughout the country to secure the nomination of President Lincoln render necessary some counteraction on the part of those unconditional friends of the Union who differ from the policy of his administration.

So long as no efforts were made to forestall the political action of the people, it was both wise and patriotic for all true friends of the Government to devote their influence to the suppression of the rebellion. But when it becomes evident that party machinery and official influence are being used to secure the perpetuation of the present administration, those who conscientiously believe that the interests of the country and of freedom demand a change in favor of rigor and purity and nationality have no choice but to appeal at once to the people, before it shall be too late to secure a fair discussion of principles.

Those in behalf of whom this communication is made have thoughtfully surveyed the political field, and have arrived at the following conclusions:

1. That even were the reëlection of Mr. Lincoln desirable, it is practically impossible against the union of influences which will oppose him.

2. That should he be reëlected his manifest tendency toward compromises and temporary expedients of policy will become stronger during a second term that it had been in the first, and the cause of human liberty and the dignity and honor of the nation suffer proportionately; while the war may continue to languish during his whole administration, till the public debt shall become a burden too great to be borne.

3. That the patronage of the Government, through the necessities of the war, has been so rapidly increased, and to such an enormous extent, and so loosely placed, as to render the application of the "one-term principle" absolutely essential to the certain safety of our republican institutions.

4. That we find united in Hon. Salmon P. Chase more of the qualities needed in a President during the next four years than are combined in any other available candidate. His record is clear and unimpeachable, showing him to be a statesman of rare ability and an administrator of the very highest order; while his private character furnishes the surest obtainable guaranty of economy and purity in the management of public affairs.

5. That the discussion of the Presidential question, already commenced by the friends of Mr. Lincoln, has developed a popularity and strength in Mr. Chase unexpected even to his warmest admirers; and, while we are aware that this strength is at present unorganized and in no condition to manifest its real magnitude, we are satisfied that it only needs systematic and faithful effort to develop it to an extent sufficient to overcome all opposing obstacles.

For these reasons the friends of Mr. Chase have determined upon measures which shall present his claims fairly and at once to the country. A central organization has been effected, which already has its connections in all the States, and the object of which is to enable his friends everywhere most effectually to promote his elevation to the Presidency. We wish the hearty coöperation of all those in favor of a speedy restoration of the Union upon the basis of universal freedom, and who desire an administration of the Government, during the first period of its new life, which shall to the fullest extent develop the capacity of free institutions, enlarge the resources of the country, diminish the burdens of taxation, elevate the standard of public and private morality, vindicate the honor of the republic before the world, and in all things make our American nationality the fairest example for imitation which human progress has ever achieved.

If these objects meet your approval, you can render efficient aid by exerting yourself at once to organize your section of the country, and by corresponding with the Chairman of the National Executive Committee, for the purpose either of receiving or imparting information.

Very respectfully,

S. C. POMEROY,
Chairman National Executive Committee.

The Pomeroy intrigue, by whomever instituted, proved a failure, and after the pronounced opinion of the Republicans of Ohio and New Hampshire, Mr. Chase, as already stated, became convinced that any effort in his behalf at that time would be to his injury. He therefore gave up the question, and made known that in doing so he "considered it more a privilege than a duty, and that no further consideration be given to his name." A few days later, Pomeroy—in open Senate—in a prepared speech defending and explaining the circular, denied that it was secret, delivered a high eulogium on the Secretary of the Treasury, and notwithstanding Mr. Chase proposed to withdraw his name, declared, "We still believe him to be the man whom the people will delight to honor," because, among other reasons, his election would insure "the *confiscation* of the property of leading rebels, and the organization, in the disloyal States, of a *republican form of government*," and "such *subordination of States* to the general Government as shall secure a *true nationality*." These were the motives which impelled the radical movement against the reëlection of Mr. Lincoln, the key to the radical demonstration, and the groundwork of their opposition to him. Other topics, such as "the immediate crushing out of the rebellion by every power in the Government, *without amnesty proclamations*," "Constitutional amendments abolishing and for ever prohibiting slavery," the "Monroe doctrine," "rigid economy," "a sound system of national currency," the "one-term policy," the "protective system" and "aid toward the construction of a Pacific railroad," were incidental questions, on most of which all sections of the Republican party were agreed.

President Lincoln was pronounced too lenient—not sufficiently severe—was not proscriptive toward the rebels; sought to induce them to return to duty by kindness and amnesty, which the extreme Republicans disapproved and the radicals denounced; he had issued emancipation and amnesty proclamations, but the radicals, who denied that the three great departments of the Government were independent, and claimed that the Executive was subordinate to the Legislature, wanted more than an Executive order—a measure of war necessity—insisted that the President could not act until he obtained the assent of Congress, and required an amendment of the Constitution abolishing slavery. Moreover, behind all this were latent purposes, which the radicals did not avow and make attest, because the place-politicians, with whom they affiliated, were not then prepared to go full length with them. These were the enfranchisement of the negroes, conferring upon them, by federal authority, the privilege of voting in the elections, and a proscription and subjugation of the intelligent whites, with the subversion of the State governments, involving the absorption of the States and conversion of our federal system into a more consolidated government, with supreme central power. These were important objects of Thad. Stevens, H. Winter Davis, and the master spirits of the radicals. Pomeroy, whose name is appended to the circular, acted, as he declared in open Senate, in behalf of "the National Committee"—a self-constituted committee, "composed of members of Congress and other citizens," of whom he was one, and was a co-laborer and willing instrument. This committee issued the "letter—called by some a circular—which he said was not private or secret, for it was sent by mail" to "distinguished persons."

The President was apprised of secret meetings of some of his professed friends in Congress, and their radical associates, who had in view a change of administration and of the policy of the Government, by substituting a new candidate for the office of Chief Magistrate in the approaching election. While he could not otherwise than feel unpleasant at these intrigues, which were more hostile to the policy that he believed best for the country than to himself personally, he took no direct steps to counteract them, but remained a passive though not inattentive observer of the artifices and schemes of these quondam friends.

That he was aware of the movements against him I did not

doubt, though for a time he studiously avoided alluding to party electioneering which concerned himself. But in a conversation of a general character with myself and two or three others—about the time that the call of the Republican National Committee in February was issued—when the intrigues that were active against him were mentioned, he said he had been informed of them, and that circulars—which were to be privately circulated—had been prepared, but were not yet signed; one had been put into his hands. He had not read it, and said he probably never should. There was doubtless more or less personality, which he always avoided. He understood, however, that issue was taken to the policy which he was pursuing in regard to the rebel States and their restoration to the Union, to which the men engaged in getting up this circular were opposed. This was, he believed, the chief objection to the Administration; and if they sincerely believed a different policy was best for the country, and would bring about union and peace, it was probably a duty on their part to try and effect a change. It was impossible for him to engage in any persecuting scheme against the erring people who had undertaken to secede from the Union. He had no desire to kill them, to exile them, to subjugate them, to confiscate their property, or deprive them of their legal and constitutional rights for mistaken views or even for their criminal conduct. "A great wrong, originating in political differences, has been committed, by which we and they are sufferers. The question is, Are we ever again to be united and fellow countrymen? If so, there is, by my theory, much to forgive. Those who are in this new movement seem to think there is nothing to forget. I am for conciliation: they seem to be governed by resentments. They believe we can be made one people by force and vengeance: I think we are not likely to bring about unity by hatred and persecution. If there is really this difference, our paths are different, and there is no necessity for secrecy or concealment."

No mention was made of candidates, nor was there direct allusion to any individual, by the President or either of the gentlemen present, though doubtless each of them had the same persons in view. When the circular was published Mr.

Chase was announced as embodying all the requisite qualifications for an efficient Chief Magistrate; and the reëlection of Mr. Lincoln, who had them not, was denounced as a practical impossibility.

On the 22d of February the National Committee, which had been appointed in Chicago in 1860, issued a call for a Republican national convention to nominate candidates for President and Vice-President. The committee designated Baltimore as the place, and the 7th of June as the time, for the meeting of this convention. Extraordinary efforts were made, particularly by the friends of Mr. Chase, to induce the committee to postpone the convention to a later period; but having the welfare of the country and the success of the Republican party in view, they acted upon their own convictions, irrespective of factious or personal aspirants, or the well meaning but mistaken advice of individuals. This call, with the unquestioned preference of the Republicans in the several States for Mr. Lincoln, satisfied many, if not all the radicals, that the renomination of the President could not be at that time easily prevented. Some very worthy gentlemen, who had become interested for Mr. Chase—as well as some men not so worthy—were nevertheless unwilling to relinquish their preference for that gentleman, and still less willing to accept Mr. Lincoln for a second term. They therefore, in the latter part of March—after Mr. Chase's letter and Pomeroy's circular had been published, and after the speech in the Senate explaining and defending the circular—addressed a formal and earnest communication to the Republican National Executive Committee, urging a postponement of the nominating convention until September. W. C. Bryant—the veteran politician and poet, a friend of Mr. Chase—was persuaded to head this letter. The reasons, as set forth by these gentlemen, for postponement, were, the importance of union in support of a single candidate, and acquiescence in the nomination when made—with an assertion that unanimity could be obtained so early as June; a declaration that the continuance of the existing administration or a change of leaders depended on the measures pursued during the spring and summer; and an opinion or intimation that postponement would allay the acrimony of Presidential strife. The committee thus addressed were not only not convinced, but, with one exception, took an entirely different view from that presented by the distinguished gentlemen, as regarded the expediency of postponement, and dissented entirely from the correctness of the reasons urged for delay. They were aware—though some of the gentlemen who addressed them probably were not—that there had been intrigues and secret meetings of the radicals, the discontented, and the aspiring for many months, with a view of displacing or supplanting Mr. Lincoln; that while he and his friends were occupied in carrying on the Government and prosecuting the war successfully, the malcontents of the Republican party, of every shade, were making common cause against the President, and exerting themselves to create a prejudice, in the Republican party, against the Administration. The very object of some of the gentlemen who urged delay was to make diversion and gain time to promote dissension and discord, which might tend to the advantage of their favorites. The President was a mark against whom the shafts of all the disaffected Republicans, as well as the peace Democrats, were directed. This the Committee, better than their advisers, well understood, and therefore wisely declined to listen to the suggestions and recommendations of the respectable gentlemen who appealed to them for delay.

When it was conclusively ascertained that the Executive Committee would not postpone the meeting of the convention, and that it would assemble in June, a scheme to forestall and embarrass it was adopted. Early in May a call for a convention, to meet at Cleveland on the 31st of that month, appeared, signed by a large number, who styled themselves "The People's Provisional Committee," at the head of which was B. Gratz Brown, the youthful Senator from Missouri. Some forty or fifty prominent men, of active and extreme political views, constituted this People's Provisional Committee. By whom they were appointed and for whom they were authorized to act, was not stated. They appeared to be self-appointed. The primary cause assigned for this proceeding was the danger to be apprehended from the patronage of the Government, and the devotion of the People's Provisional Committee to the principle of one term; opposition to a national convention at Baltimore, by reason of its proximity to the centre of all the interested influences of the Administration; the distance of that place from the centre of the country; and a conviction that there should be a central position indicated, to which every one might go and express his individual opinions and preferences. This call was of a central and consolidating character—an appeal in behalf of personal, not State rights; putting aside the federal features of the Government, and making it entirely central. Almost simultaneously with this appeal another call was published, signed by about an equal number of persons, from different parts of the country. At the head of them was Lucius Robinson, a prominent politician of New York, since elected Governor of that State. These gentlemen invited the citizens of the United States, who meant to uphold the Union and suppress the rebellion, without infringing the rights of individuals or of States, and who were for amending the Federal Constitution so as to exclude slavery, to meet in mass convention at Cleveland on the 31st of May. Still another call was issued, by the Central Fremont Club and others, for those who were for the "immediate extinction of slavery by *Congressional* action, and for the absolute equality of all men before the law, without regard to race or color, and such a plan of reconstruction as shall conform to the policy of freedom for all, placing the political power alone in the hands of the loyal, and executing with vigor the law for *confiscating* the property of all rebels," to also assemble at Cleveland on the 31st of May.

This last call declared the Cleveland convention was convoked in consequence of "the imbecile and vacillating policy of the present Administration in the conduct of the war, being just weak enough to waste its men and means, to provoke the enemy, but not strong enough to conquer the rebellion; and its treachery to justice, freedom, and genuine democratic principles in its plan of reconstruction, whereby the honor and dignity of the nation have been sacrificed to conciliate the still existing and arrogant slave power, and to further the ends of an unscrupulous partisan ambition, call in thunder tones upon the lovers of justice and their country to come to the rescue of the imperilled nationality and the cause of impartial justice and uni-

versal freedom, threatened with betrayal and overthrow. The
way to victory and salvation is plain. Justice must be throned in
the seat of national legislation and guide the national will."

After the assassination of Lincoln language like this was
applied by the radicals, who had then obtained control of
"national legislation," to President Johnson, who adhered to and
maintained the Lincoln "plan of reconstruction," and suffered
impeachment from a radical House of Representatives for his
honesty and fidelity to the Constitution.

These several calls, differing in phraseology, and specifying
in some respects different purposes, were well known to be
but parts of one great intrigue. It was a concerted scheme by
a few individuals some of whom had a personal preference for
another candidate than Mr. Lincoln—whose efforts for peace and
union, they thought, were too mild toward the rebels—but the
moving spirits, whose designs were most dangerous and are
most apparent in the last of the above calls, intended not only
a change of administration, but of the structure of the Government. Many, doubtless a majority of those who gave their names
to these several calls for a meeting of factions, on the 31st of
May, at Cleveland, were unaware of the radical efforts to effect,
by a political party election, a revolution—the subversion of our
federal system and the establishment of a central consolidated
power that should be supreme and absolute over the States
and also regulate the local affairs of the country and people.
The names of the principal scheming managers and prompters in
this revolutionary purpose do not appear in either of these
calls—they were studiously withheld. Although the movement
was vigorous and active, and the machinery put in operation
was extensive, the Cleveland convention or conventions were
each and all abortions. There was quite a gathering of wayward,
impracticable, and theoretical minds, with crude, fanatical, and
strange ideas of government and of the fundamental law—men
with wild notions of liberty and equality, and of State and personal rights. Some were possessed of an absurd and ridiculous
conception of the power and authority of the federal executive,
and seemed ignorant of the constitutional limitations of the

federal Government, and with them all was a substratum of hate and vengeance under the cloak of philanthropy and patriotism. Before these conventions assembled the intelligent friends of Mr. Chase and that gentleman himself became aware of the motley, incongruous, and heterogeneous materials of which that gathering was composed, and he persisted in declining to have his name presented or used. Some of the malcontents from the start were opposed to him, and wanted a more avowed radical candidate—one who had not been connected with the Lincoln administration. The result was the nomination of John C. Fremont, with a series of resolutions less offensive in the main than might have been expected from such a gathering; but a reconstruction of the Union—virtually a change of the governments, State and federal—and a confiscation of the property of the rebels, were insisted upon as fundamental. These were the purposes and tendencies of many in that stormy era, and really the great ends sought by the radical leaders.

General Fremont promptly accepted the nomination, and as a manifestation of his sincerity and confidence in the success of the movement forthwith resigned his commission of Major General in the army to put himself, without embarrassment, at the head. In his letter of acceptance he admitted that he should subject himself to the reproach of creating a schism in the party, but his justification was the alleged infidelity of Mr. Lincoln to the principles he was elected to defend, which infidelity, Fremont said, had first created the schism. The Administration he denounced as marked by a disregard of constitutional rights and violations of personal liberty and the liberty of the press, with other monstrous wrongs. Against the disastrous condition of affairs brought on, he said, by Mr. Lincoln, Fremont declared the Cleveland convention which nominated him was a protest. He took occasion, however, to express his non-concurrence in some of the fantastical and violent measures of the convention. He especially objected to a confiscation of all rebel property. He also dissented from the spirit of vengeance manifested, because it would not be likely to secure permanent peace, nor was it consistent with the happiness and general

tranquillity of the whole country, which were sought by all. If
the Baltimore convention in June would nominate any man
whose past life would justify a well-grounded confidence in his
fidelity to Republican principles, there was, Fremont said, no
reason why there should be division. But if Mr. Lincoln was
nominated, it would be fatal to the country.

A portion of the radicals had from the first preferred Fremont to Chase, and the more earnest thought him a preferable
candidate until they read his letter of acceptance, which disgusted extremists like Wade, Thad. Stevens, and H. Winter
Davis, whose policy was unqualifiedly for confiscation, subjugation, and vengeance. Others, from different causes, began to
doubt, lose interest, became lax and indifferent, and the Cleveland ticket, which had not much strength to begin with, grew
more feeble from the day it was made public. If Fremont would
not confiscate—if he would not overturn the governments of
the Southern States, convert them into territories, and persecute
and subjugate the Southern whites, he was, in the estimation of
the radicals, little better than Lincoln. The Treasury agents,
a mercenary legion, lost interest when Chase was withdrawn;
and most of the instigators wilted in zeal and the vast machinery
which had been employed in getting up the several Cleveland
conventions became useless. The seeds of dissatisfaction which
had been extensively sown, were not, however, utterly destroyed,
but still retained vitality.

Although Mr. Chase had publicly declined being a candidate,
his friends or supporters did not wholly discontinue their
efforts in his behalf, nor was he displeased with their persistency.
They were opposed to Mr. Lincoln, and had persuaded themselves that if the nominating convention could be postponed
until autumn, they could, by labor and other appliances, effect
his defeat, and probably secure the selection of the Secretary
of the Treasury as his successor. Their efforts for delay were
consequently extensive and immense. Governor Morgan of
New York, chairman of the Republican National Committee,
to whom these appeals for postponement were chiefly addressed, was so much annoyed by them, and so much disturbed by the calls from numerous and respectable sources,

from every part of the country, as to become alarmed, and felt that the responsibility was too great for him to refuse without support. He wrote me on the 10th of May to name the month to which I would postpone the convention if I desired a postponement. The request was a surprise, for we had both, in repeated interviews, previously concurred on this subject, and the machinery which prompted these apparently spontaneous demonstrations among Republicans was so transparent, that my answer was immediate and decisive against any delay, for by it the malcontents had everything to gain and nothing to lose. It would give the intriguers and opponents of the President weeks to assail and misrepresent him, and compel his friends to defend him against the assaults, when they could be otherwise better and more usefully employed. Two days after my answer Governor Morgan informed me that he knew my opinion, but had, in self-defence, before addressing me, sent a similar inquiry to every member of the committee, and that every man, except Mr. Spooner of Ohio, had returned an answer similar to mine, but Spooner was for a postponement. This was indicative of the source of the movement and of the influence of Mr. Chase.

The delegates to the Republican national convention assembled at Baltimore on the 7th of June, pursuant to the original call. It was composed mainly of judicious and discreet men, who possessed, and generally deserved, the confidence of the patriotic and loyal citizens whom they represented and for whom they acted. Two sets of delegates appeared from Missouri, and the convention awarded seats to those styling themselves the radical Union delegation, though aware of the discontent of these persons, and their hostility to President Lincoln, the Administration, and the policy of the Government. But if factious and extremists, they probably represented a majority of the Republicans of Missouri, of that date, where the fratricidal warfare had been ferocious and vindictive beyond any other State. The people there had felt the evils of the terrible conflict, and the radicals, fired with resentment, were unforgiving and unrelenting toward not only the rebels, but those Republicans who were not as intolerant and vindictive as themselves.

While the convention was not in sympathy with this unsparing and persecuting element, it recognized and accepted the majority principle, and so decided.

On the ballot for President Mr. Lincoln received the unanimous vote of every State but Missouri. That delegation was so opposed to him and his policy as to refuse at first to favor his renomination. Nor were they satisfied with General Fremont, who opposed the radical policy of confiscation and vengeance. They therefore cast the vote of that State for General U. S. Grant.

On the question of Vice-President there was diversity of opinion. Mr. Hamlin, who was elected with Mr. Lincoln in 1860, had not displayed that breadth of view and enlightened statesmanship which was expected, and consequently lost confidence with the country during his term, yet there was no concentration or unity on any one to fill his place. His friends and supporters, while conscious that he brought no strength to the ticket, claimed, but with no great zeal or earnestness, that as Mr. Lincoln was renominated, it would be invidious not to renominate Hamlin also.

The question of substituting another for Vice-President had been discussed in political circles prior to the meeting of the convention, without any marked personal preference, but with a manifest desire that there should be a change. Mr. Lincoln felt the delicacy of his position, and was therefore careful to avoid the expression of any opinion; but it was known to those who enjoyed his confidence that he appreciated the honesty, integrity, and self-sacrificing patriotism of Andrew Johnson of Tennessee. There were, moreover, circumstances, political and local, that commended Johnson. He was a Democrat in his antecedents, was a citizen of a slave State, who alone, of all the Senators of the South, had fearlessly resisted secession. Beyond almost any public man he had been a sufferer for his fidelity to the Constitution and the Union, was proscribed, and with his family had been exiled from his home. He had been found ever true and reliable—self-sacrificing and faithful in the cause of his country. A large portion of the members, but not a majority of the convention, were impressed with

these facts from the commencement, and as they were considered and discussed the sentiment in his favor became almost
universal. When the ballot took place he received two hundred
votes, a majority of fifty over Hamlin. An immediate change
took place with those who had not at first supported him,
and the final result was that of the 520 votes cast, Johnson
received 494—and his nomination was made unanimous.

Questions arose in the convention as to the reception of
the delegates who presented themselves as the representatives
of the Union people of Tennessee, Arkansas, and Louisiana,
and claimed equal rights, and privileges with the delegates of
the other States. This subject involved the principle of restoration, reconstruction, and reunion, which had been agitated for
two years in Congress, and was a dividing line between the
radicals and the conservative Republicans. The convention, by
a vote of about two to one, decided to admit them. This decision was received as an affirmation and endorsement of the
Lincoln policy of conciliation and reconstruction, which the
radicals in Congress, under the lead of Wade, Sumner, and
Stevens, at a later day defeated. Those States, with others, after
the rebellion was suppressed, and after the death of Lincoln,
were under the administration of Johnson denied representation by the radical majority in Congress, and excluded from
their undoubted constitutional rights in the republic.

The radical leaders, finding themselves unable to stem
the overwhelming popular current in favor of Mr. Lincoln, sought
to defeat his conciliatory policy. Not content with putting down
the insurrection, and maintaining the integrity of the Union,
they insisted on the subjugation and vindictive punishment of
the rebels by overthrowing their State governments, confiscating
their property, depriving them of their homes, giving their lands
to the conquering soldiers, and thus colonizing the South with
a new population from the North and West. Outside influences were brought to bear on the convention and the President,
to induce a change of measures by prominent radicals who
gathered at Baltimore, aided by the "National Union League
of America," a secret party organization composed chiefly of men
of ultra views. This league met in Baltimore, by their Grand

Council, simultaneously with the Republican convention, and sought to make themselves felt by a series of resolutions, which were presented to the President by the league on the same day that he was informed of his renomination by the convention. The country, it was expected, would receive these resolutions as a part of the proceedings at Baltimore, and have effect by being published with them. The most marked of them, intended as a rebuke and stimulant, resolved, "That the confiscation acts of Congress should be promptly and vigorously enforced, and that homesteads on the lands confiscated under it should be granted to our soldiers, who have been made indigent by the acts of traitors and rebels."

This atrocious scheme of plunder and robbery, by which the Southern people were to be deprived of their homes and driven into exile, had for some time been pressed upon the President, who was not a convert to its justice or a believer that union, peace, and good will could be by such a policy restored. Though adopted by the Union League, and formally presented with an address, the monstrous proposition was to him no novelty. Thurlow Weed, the party manager of a not very scrupulous organization in New York, but who possessed a certain influence in that State, had in personal interviews urged this scheme, and in a private letter to the President, on the 8th of November, 1863, elaborated a plan, advising the President to "issue a proclamation announcing that in the future prosecution of the war, the maintenance of the Government, and the preservation of the Union, all territory, whether it be farms, plantations, villages or cities, shall be partitioned equitably between and among the officers and soldiers by whom it shall have been conquered."

This vandal proposition, from such a quarter, earnestly pressed, disturbed but did not influence the President in 1863, nor did its renewal by so formidable a combination as the "National Union League of America," in 1864, accompanying his nomination and pending the Presidential election, convince him or extort his acquiescence. Confiscation, especially general confiscation, had at no time been a favorite project with the President, and when coupled with a scheme to expel the inhabitants from their homes, was of such a demoralizing and bar-

barous character as to receive not his approval, but his abhorrence. The author of this vicious scheme, in submitting it to the President in 1863, gravely stated it would secure an abundance of military recruits—"enterprising yeomen"—who would "have an intelligent reason for entering the army, and who would know that the realization of their hopes depends upon their zeal, fidelity, and courage. And by thus providing homes and occupations when the war is over for our disbanded soldiers, you have scattered over rebel territory an element that may be relied upon for reconstruction of civil government in the seceded States."

The proposed appeal to the cupidity and malignity of the people did not favorably impress the President. Our armies were not made up of mere mercenary soldiers, fighting for Southern farms and homes, but of patriotic men who battled for their country and their rights. It was not a war for disunion, nor yet for exclusion.

When the war terminated there were dispersed through the South a needy set of adventurers, not inaptly termed "carpet-baggers," who, if they were not endowed with the confiscated farms and homes of the Southern people, according to the radical programme, contrived to seize the offices, lay heavy taxes, and for years appropriated to themselves a large portion of the revenues of those States. This they were enabled to do, and to misgovern the people, in the subdued and enfeebled condition of those commonwealths, by an extraordinary exercise of federal power, by a radical majority in Congress, enforced by federal arms.

It was not by means and methods like these that President Lincoln and the Administration expected to effect conciliation and a restoration of the Union. The Republican convention in renominating him adopted his policy. The National Union League of America asserted the radical policy to which he could not subscribe. To the delegations from each body which tendered him congratulations and support he expressed his gratification that he was thought not unworthy to be entrusted with the place which he had occupied for the last three years. While he expressed his assent to and approval of the resolutions of the Republican convention, he passed by the resolutions of the league, which had been skilfully prepared and were presented to him on the same day, and concluded his brief remarks to that delegation by saying: "I do not allow myself to suppose that either the convention or the league has concluded to decide that I am either the greatest or best man in America, but rather they have concluded that it is not best to swap horses while crossing the river, and have further concluded that I am not so poor a horse, that they might not make a botch of it in trying to swap."

I am not aware that the President ever made other comment on the Cleveland attempt to swap horses, or allusion to the assaults of Fremont, than the above anecdotal remark in reply to the radical delegates of the Loyal League.

7

Administration of Abraham Lincoln, V

> Lincoln's troubles in 1864 were not over with his nomina-
> tion. The bitter Wade-Davis Manifesto which followed
> was a sign of the dissatisfaction of the radicals who
> hoped to displace the President even after he had become
> the official candidate of his party. How Lincoln over-
> came these difficulties, how he made plans for a vigorous
> prosecution of the war even in case of an election defeat,
> constitute the topics of this essay.

THE YEAR 1864 was one of severe trial to President Lincoln.
For nearly three years from his inauguration he had put forth
his strength and that of the Government in the mighty struggle
to preserve the national integrity against dismemberment, and
had, while resisting the sectional efforts of the South to dissolve
the Union, encountered persistent opposition from the Democratic party organization of the North. Besides these difficulties,
the radical element of the Republican party, comprising the
more enthusiastic as well as the most violent politicians in prosecuting the war, had become dissatisfied with the conciliatory
policy of the Administration and the slow progress of our
armies. Some victories had been achieved, but they seemed barren
of results, and the radical leaders in Congress availed themselves
of this fact, and also of the murmurs and complaints that the
war was unreasonably protracted, to promote greater discontent.

The President was held responsible for delays and military
mismanagement, and the approaching Presidential election served
as a stimulant to the dissatisfied spirits, who began to crystallize

The Galaxy, XXIV (December, 1877)

into an organization. The radicals, as zealous party politicians as
they were patriots, began to cast about for a candidate more
arbitrary and severe than Mr. Lincoln, who was represented as
soft-hearted, and not sufficiently energetic for such a war. The
intrigues instituted in the autumn became active in the winter
and spring, and, to the annoyance of the President, one of the
Cabinet, a member of his political family, the Secretary of the
Treasury, was quietly attending some of the meetings of the
disaffected, and for a time became identified with them, and
a prominent candidate to lead them.

The assaults of open opponents, and the calumnies of professed friends, circulated often by petty officials, the President
did not regard; but he was affected by the course of the Secretary of the Treasury, to whom he had given his confidence.
Without any intention or thought of change in the financial
officer of the Administration, he never considered himself or the
Administration dependent on any one individual for its permanency or success, but was intimate and confidential with all
of them. The political principles and general governmental
views of Mr. Chase, as exemplified during his Senatorial career,
and maintained in the conduct of the administration of his
department and support of the Government, during the first
half of Mr. Lincoln's term, had favorably impressed the President, who himself, after entering upon his duties as Chief
Magistrate, became more attached to the federal system, and more
convinced of the necessity of a rigid observance of both the
granted and limited powers of the Government under the Constitution.

The President and the Secretary of the Treasury, and indeed
the whole Cabinet, though opposed to slavery, recognized and
strictly adhered to the principle of non-interference with slavery
in the States. Mr. Chase distinctly stated this in a letter of September, 1861, to Green Adams, when he said:

> I am sure that neither the President nor any member of
> of the Administration has any desire to convert this war
> for the Union and for national existence in the Union, and
> under the Constitution, into a war upon any State insti-
> tution.

This is a correct statement as regards the entire Administration in 1861. But a year later the President, under the pressure of military necessity, found it essential for the successful prosecution of the war and the salvation of the Government, to issue his preliminary proclamation of September 22, 1862, for the emancipation of slaves in the rebel States—a bold measure, devised, decided upon, and adopted by himself, as he declared when he read the document to his full Cabinet, and for it and its consequences he then and there avowed that he alone was responsible.

To Mr. Chase, the recognized, distinctive anti-slavery man of the Cabinet, the proceeding was wholly unexpected. He was, of course, not unfavorable to emancipation, but its advocate, and had not doubted that war would secure it. He anticipated, however, that it would be effected gradually and by military successes. The stops taken by Fremont in Missouri, Hunter at Port Royal, and others, to give freedom to the slaves within the lines of the Union armies, which the President disapproved, were not condemned by Chase. His suppositions and convictions were that the generals, as they made advances, would, from military necessity, give freedom to the bondmen. With a belief that through a work of detail the results would be certain, he had encouraged that policy.

Fremont's unauthorized proceeding led to that officer's being relieved of his command, and Hunter's emancipation order was revoked by the President in a proclamation of May 19, 1862, disowning any knowledge of the act—proclaiming that neither General Hunter, nor any other commander, was authorized to declare the slaves of any State free—that whether the President, as Commander-in-Chief of the army and navy, was competent to do it, might be questioned; but if it became a necessity indispensable to the maintenance of the Government to exercise such power, he, under his responsibility, reserved to himself its exercise, and that he did not feel justified in leaving the decision to commanders in the field.

When, in September, 1862, the war had made such progress as to render interference by the general Government necessary, he did not leave the subject to subordinates, but took upon him-

self the responsibility alluded to in his proclamation of May. Mr.
Chase had the sagacity to see that the prestige previously ac-
corded him as the leading emancipationist of the Administration
would thereafter cease. What he had expected would be brought
about in detail by the generals in their progress upon rebel territories, the President, as Commander-in-Chief, had by one bold
stroke accomplished under the war powers. Emancipation, as
decreed by Mr. Lincoln, was not a legislative enactment, a
statutory law under the Constitution, but an Executive order,
the result of military necessity—an act of the President as Commander-in-Chief in the prosecution of the war rather than in his
civil administrative capacity as Chief Magistrate, striking down
at one blow one of the most sacred and specially guarded of all
the rights which the States had reserved to themselves. It was
claimed, however, and by none more strenuously than by some of
the radicals in Congress, that it was a high-handed assumption;
that while they were favorable to emancipation, legislation was
necessary to consummate the measure. Yet in truth neither the
legislative nor the executive branch, nor both combined, were
constitutionally empowered to emancipate—it was purely a war
measure, and of its necessity the President had to judge, and take
the responsibility. If the Executive could do this, why, asked
the radicals, had not he and Congress power to go still further
with the rebels and rebel States, and modify their institutions in
other respects? Why not protect the slaves when free—endow
them with suffrage, and though ignorant and uncultured, make
them by law politically the equals of the whites, who were
cultured and refined? The answer was those would be civil
acts, and did not come under the laws of war or military
necessity. But the radicals insisted that Congress could emancipate without regard for the Constitution, or considering the
change which this assumption would effect in our federal system—making the general Government supervisory and absolute
over the States and people—a government of persons regulating
and dictating the social and political condition of the people, en-
forcing by law equality of the races, overruling local sovereignties, and absorbing and exercising powers never delegated.

Senator Sumner, who seemed to consider himself the patron

and special guardian of the colored race, and particularly of the slaves, early claimed that Government aid and protection must be given to the negroes, whom he styled "wards of the nation," and the States compelled to allow them to vote. Mr. Chase earnestly supported the President's emancipation policy, but did not at once assent to the centralizing theories of Sumner and the extremists. A regard for the reserved sovereignty of the States and the principle of strict construction which he had previously maintained, gave way after the President's emancipation proclamation, and he coöperated with Senator Sumner in the policy of excluding the rebel States from the Union, and denying them restoration until the negroes were permitted to vote. The dissatisfaction of the leading radicals in Congress because the President had, by an executive order, without Congressional assistance, done an act which they could disapprove, was increased, and led them to cast about through the succeeding year for a Presidential candidate of less individuality to succeed Mr. Lincoln. Their minds seemed to concentrate on the Secretary of the Treasury, and he, nothing loth, was approached on the subject. While exceedingly solicitous in regard to the office, he felt the delicacy of his position, and his relation to the chief who gave him his confidence—was coy and reserved—met in secret with these uneasy spirits, but did not communicate that fact or the purpose to the President. His sentiments on the subject of being a candidate, and especially his feelings toward and his honest opinions of Mr. Lincoln, are truthfully expressed in the following private letter to his son-in-law, Governor Sprague:

WASHINGTON, NOVEMBER 26, 1863.

. . . If I were controlled by merely personal sentiments, I should prefer the reëlection of Mr. Lincoln to that of any other man. But I doubt the expediency of reëlecting anybody, and I think a man of different qualities from those the President has will be needed for the next four years. I am not anxious to be regarded as that man; and I am quite willing to leave that question to the decision of those who agree in thinking that some such man should be chosen.

I can never permit myself to be driven into any hostile or unfriendly position as to Mr. Lincoln. His course toward

me has always been so fair and kind, his progress toward entire agreement with me on the great question of slavery has
been so constant, though rather slower than I wished for,
and his general character is so marked by traits which command respect and affection, that I can never consent to
anything which he himself could or would consider as incompatible with perfect honor and good faith, if I were
capable—which I hope I am not—of a departure from either,
even where an enemy might be concerned. . . .

A few days after this letter was written, President Lincoln
issued his amnesty proclamation, extending pardon to those
rebels who would return to duty, and also inviting reconstruction and restoration. This document, intended to promote reconciliation and the reëstablishment of the suspended States in their
true position, had been thoroughly discussed in Cabinet, and
distinctly approved by every member, but was denounced by the
radicals as another Executive assumption.

The amnesty proclamation and annual message were transmitted to Congress on the 8th of December, 1863, and on the
15th of December Thaddeus Stevens moved a reference of that
part which related to the condition and treatment of the rebel
States to a special committee. This motion was amended by H.
Winter Davis, who proposed to refer that part of the message
which related to the duty of the United States to guarantee to
the States a republican form of government, to a committee
of nine. It was well understood that this movement was antagonistic to the policy of the President, and by those in the
intrigue, to the President himself. The persons concerned were
in constant intimate intercourse with the Secretary of the
Treasury, and, on the 22d of February, on the appearance of the
Pomeroy circular, three months after the letter to Governor
Sprague, Mr. Chase informed the President that he had been
consulted in regard to the selection of a person for President,
and consented himself to be a candidate.

About this time his views of amnesty and the President's
policy of extending pardon to the rebels, and a restoration of the
suspended States to the Union, appear to have undergone a

change. In a letter to Gerritt Smith on the 2d of March, 1864, when the efforts in his behalf were at the culminating point, he said:

> The amnesty proclamation seems to fail. I don't like the qualification in the oath required; nor the limitation of the right of suffrage to those who take the oath, and are otherwise qualified according to the State laws in force before the rebellion. I fear these are fatal concessions. Why should not *all* soldiers who fight for their country vote in it? Why should not the intelligent colored man of Louisiana have a voice as a free citizen in restoring and maintaining loyal ascendency?

Not until these radical meetings in the winter of 1864 to make a President do I recollect that Mr. Chase favored the policy of conferring on colored persons the privilege of voting by the exercise of federal authority, nor even then that he thought the amnesty proclamation seemed to fail.

It is due to President Lincoln and Secretary Chase to state that at a later period, and only a day or two preceding the President's death, there arose a difference as to the sentiments of Mr. Chase on some points of the amnesty proclamation. The points are of historical interest, and though the issue was raised subsequently, it may be properly introduced here.

Mr. Lincoln, on his return to Washington, after the fall of Richmond, was serenaded on the evening of the 11th of April, by his fellow citizens, whom he addressed from the portico of the White House in a carefully prepared speech. The occasion was one of deep interest, not only from the fact of the downfall of the rebellion, but from the opening future of our political condition. The crisis had arrived when it was to be decided whether his policy of conciliation, giving to the rebels amnesty, to the suspended States their proper practical relation with the Union, and to the whole country reconciliation and peace, or whether the radical policy of continued contention, subjugation, disunion of States, sectional animosity, sectional government of a part of the States by other sections, and a disregard and destruc-

tion of that political equality of the States which was guaranteed
by the Constitution, should prevail. Down to this period, when
the Confederacy was dissolving, and the war virtually at an end,
the President, who, by his ability, skill, and management, had
continued to keep the Republicans united, and in the main succeeded in carrying forward his humane and paternal policy,
was at open issue with the radicals, whose vengeful, irreconcilable,
and persecuting hatred he had defeated.

Returning triumphant from Richmond, he was more fully
than ever before convinced of the rectitude of his course and
the necessity of magnanimity to the Southern people if the
country was to be united, prosperous, and at peace. At the same
time he was aware that he would be compelled to encounter
resistance and violent opposition from the leading radical minds,
who took different views, and had party ends to subserve. It
was under these circumstances, and with a full knowledge of the
difficulties to be met in reëstablishing the Union by a restoration
of the States to their proper practical relation, that his speech of
the 11th of April was prepared. It was not an impromptu speech,
but a written document, deliberately and studiously prepared—
the last public utterance of President Lincoln on the subject of
reconstruction, which he had adopted and consistently pursued,
and which, had he not been murdered, he would, without
doubt, have carried to successful completion, but for adhering
to which his successor, not less honest and firm, but less skilful
and adroit in managing men, was impeached. President Lincoln
said:

As a general rule I abstain from reading the reports of
attacks upon myself wishing not to be provoked by that to
which I cannot properly offer an answer. In spite of this
precaution, however, it comes to my knowledge that I am
much censured from some supposed agency in setting up
and seeking to sustain the new State government of Louisiana. In this I have done just so much as and no more than
the public knows. In the annual message of December, 1863,
and accompanying proclamation, I presented a plan of reconstruction (as the phrase goes) which I promised, if
adopted by any State, should be acceptable to and sustained

by the executive government of the nation. I distinctly stated that this was not the only plan which might possibly be acceptable; and I also distinctly protested that the Executive claimed no right to say when or whether members should be admitted to seats in Congress from such States. This plan was, in advance, submitted to the then Cabinet, and distinctly approved by every member of it. One of them suggested that I should then, and in that connection, apply the emancipation proclamation to the theretofore excepted parts of Virginia and Louisiana; that I should drop the suggestion about apprenticeship for freed people, and that I should omit the protest against my own power in regard to the admission of members of Congress; but even he approved every part and parcel of the plan which has since been employed or touched by the action of Louisiana. . . .

I have been shown a letter on this subject, supposed to be an able one, in which the writer expresses regret that my mind has not seemed to be definitely fixed on the question whether the seceding States, so called, are in the Union or out of it. It would perhaps add astonishment to his regret were he to learn that, since I have found professed Union men endeavoring to make that question, I have *purposely* forborne any public expression upon it. As appears to me that question has not been, or yet is, a practically material one, and that any discussion of it, while it thus remains practically immaterial, could have no effect other than the mischievous one of dividing our friends. As yet, whatever it may hereafter become, that question is bad, as a basis of a controversy, and good for nothing at all—a merely pernicious abstraction. We all agree that the seceding States, so called, are out of their proper practical relation with the Union, and that the sole object of the Government, civil and military, in regard to those States, is to again get them into that proper practical relation. I believe it is not only possible, but in fact easier to do this without deciding, or even considering, whether these States have ever been out of the Union, than with it. Finding themselves safely at home, it would be utterly immaterial whether they had ever been abroad. Let us all join in doing the acts necessary to restoring the proper practical relations between these States and the Union, and each for ever after innocently indulge his own opinion whether, in doing the acts, he brought the States from without into the Union, or only gave them proper assistance, they never having been out of it.

President Lincoln's policy of peace and reconstruction adopted at an early day, and communicated to Congress in December, 1863, had encountered persistent opposition from the radical leaders, but from it he never swerved. It may be regarded as his unalterable conviction, and the above address his last communication to his countrymen on these subjects.

This speech, delivered on the 11th of April drew from Mr. Chase on the following day, the 12th of April, a letter, in which that gentleman said:

I recollect the suggestions you mention; my impression is that they were in writing. There was another which you do not mention, and which I think was not in writing. It is distinct in my memory, though doubtless forgotten by you. It was an objection to the restriction of participation in reorganization to persons having the qualification of voters under the laws in force just before rebellion. Ever since questions of reconstruction have been talked about it has been my opinion that colored loyalists ought to be allowed to participate in it; and it was because of this opinion that I was anxious to have this question left open. I did not, however, say much about the restriction. I was the only one who expressed a wish for its omission, and did not desire to seem pertinacious.

The extracts are characteristic of the two men, and exemplify the position and character of each.

The President was assassinated on the 14th day of April, two days after the date of Mr. Chase's letter; and this subject of difference between them terminated at his death. My own recollection of the discussion in Cabinet on the amnesty proclamation, in the autumn of 1863—particularly that which related to the subject of restricting the privilege of voting on the question of reconstruction—is in accord with that of the President. The radical opposition to that restriction, and to the President's amnesty proclamation and method of reconstruction, was immediate and active. His propositions were denounced as Executive assumptions. Stevens, Wade, H. Winter Davis, and others took instant measures to counteract and defeat them, by referring the subject to a select committee, that matured a scheme, and in February reported Davis's bill to guarantee to certain States a republican form of government.

On the 22d of February, after the publication of the Pomeroy electioneering circular, Mr. Chase, feeling it necessary to make some explanation, wrote the President, disavowing any "knowledge of the existence of the letter," but admitted that "a few weeks ago several gentlemen called on me, and expressed their desire—shared by many earnest friends of our common cause—that I would allow my name to be submitted to the consideration of the people, in convention, in connection with the approaching election of Chief Magistrate. . . . We have had several interviews. . . . I accepted their judgment as decisive. . . . The organization of the committee followed these conversations. . . . Thought this explanation due you," etc.

The explanation was not made until after the intrigue became public by the publication of Pomeroy's confidential circular; but the movement, though secret, had been known to the President almost from its inception. He replied to Mr. Chase on the 29th of February, stating:

> My knowledge of Mr. Pomeroy's letter having been made *public* came to me only the day you wrote; but I had, in in spite of myself, known of its *existence* several days before. I have not yet read it, and I think I shall not. I was not shocked or surprised by the appearance of the letter, because I had had knowledge of Mr. Pomeroy's committee, and of secret issues which, I supposed, came from it, and of secret agents who, I supposed, were sent out by it, for several weeks. I have known just as little of those things as my friends have allowed me to know. They bring the documents to me, but I do not read them; they tell me what they think fit to tell me, but I do not inquire for more.

Mr. Chase resigned his place in the Treasury, after the nomination at Baltimore, and left the Department on the 30th of

June—the close of the fiscal year. There had been for some time
constrained courtesy, or want of that cordial intimacy which
existed prior to 1864. The President was aware that Treasury
officials were among his sharpest opponents, and that in Congress as well as in the Treasury exception was taken to his
management of affairs and his method of administering the
Government. It was also circulated that he was under improper
influences—alluding to the Secretary of State. Mr. Lincoln was
declared by the radicals to be too yielding in his disposition; was
granting too liberal amnesty to the rebels; was for too easy reconstruction; wanted firmness; and was in fact unequal to the
vast and responsible duties of Chief Magistrate at such an important period. If these complaints or rumors were not prompted
by the Secretary of the Treasury, as was said by his opponents,
they were not checked or discountenanced by him. Some of the
most offensive objections to the President emanated from subordinates of the Treasury Department—the personal confidants
and official dependents of the Secretary. They asserted, moreover,
that the Treasury and finances were in such a condition that the
system inaugurated by Mr. Chase was necessary to the administration of the Treasury and the stability of the Government,
and that he was indispensable for its successful operation.

It was at this juncture, and with these warnings to the President and the country, that Mr. Chase tendered his resignation.
It was, as unexpectedly to himself as others, promptly accepted;
for he had, on one or two previous occasions, suggested resignation, a proposition which the President quietly put aside. The
occasion and alleged cause for this resignation was a difference
in regard to the person to be appointed assistant treasurer at
New York. Mr. John J. Cisco, the incumbent, who resigned from
infirm health, was a Democrat, and there were difficulties in
selecting a successor; but the Secretary, after canvassing many
names, finally recommended his assistant in the Department,
Maunsell B. Field, who had at one time been associated with
Mr. Cisco, and who was also a Democrat. The selection was
exceedingly distasteful to Senator Morgan and sundry prominent
Republicans, who objected to the appointment because they desired, as the Secretary feared and said, "to make a party engine

of the office, without sufficient regard for the necessities of the service." The apprehensions of the Secretary may have been unfounded in this instance; but there is no doubt that the interference of members of Congress to control appointments is often highly detrimental to good Government. In the scramble to get Congressional support for this important Executive appointment at New York—an appointment for the correct management of which the Secretary and not members of Congress was held responsible—Mr. Field succeeded in obtaining a majority of the New York members in his favor and this was claimed to be conclusive. But the President, who personally knew Mr. Field, did not think him a proper man for the place. Other circumstances not likely influenced him to decline accepting the Secretary's selection, though he usually acquiesced in the nominations of subordinates by heads of departments to places for the proper management of which they were more immediately responsible. Meantime, Mr. Cisco, on the earnest appeal of the Secretary, consented to hold the office for another quarter; and Mr. Chase, when communicating this fact, which he did on the day following the refusal to appoint Mr. Field, tendered his resignation, because, he said, "I cannot help feeling that my position here is not altogether acceptable to you." The resignation was an important step for both himself and the President; and the announcement that it had been tendered and was accepted was a surprise to the friends of both and to the country.

Governor Tod of Ohio was offered the place, but declined it. The office was then conferred on Senator Fessenden of Maine. That gentleman, though gratified with the honor, entered upon the duties with doubt and reluctance. He was, at the time—and had been from the commencement of Mr. Lincoln's administration—chairman of the Finance Committee, which brought him into close intimacy with Mr. Chase, and was a warm supporter of that gentleman and his financial policy. He had ceased to be a supporter of Mr. Seward, whom he had once admired, but was not antagonistic to Mr. Lincoln. As a lawyer Mr. Fessenden stood well at the bar; as a Senator he had exhibited capacity, and possessed legislative experience; but he was physically and often mentally dyspeptic; and, though honest and conservative, was, in his infirm health, at times afflicted with an irritable temper that impaired his usefulness. He was nevertheless recognized as occupying a place in the front rank of the Senate of that day, where he was faithful and industrious. If not always profound, he had quick perceptions, and was an excellent critic; but his political views were tainted in some degree with the prejudice of early partisanship, of which he could not always entirely divest himself. Yet he was ever desirous to be just. It was a trial to him to undertake the laborious duties of the Treasury; and in resigning his seat in the Senate to enter upon those duties, he was actuated by patriotic motives, and a willingness to make any sacrifice for his country. It was soon obvious, however, to his friends and himself, that his mind and temperament were not as well adapted to his new position as to that which he had resigned; that, whatever might be his legislative capacity, which was in many respects second to few of his associates, he was deficient in executive power and administrative skill and ability.

The retirement of Mr. Chase did not create the sensation that was anticipated. His administration of the Treasury and the finances had been so violently assailed by the Democrats, that they were compelled to accept his withdrawal as a relief; and the friends of the President, who had witnessed with disfavor the efforts to supersede Mr. Lincoln, were not sorry that Mr. Chase was disconnected with the Administration.

Sagacious men were unable to form an opinion as to the financial policy of the President in these Treasury appointments. The truth was, he had none, and did not profess to have any. Overwhelmed with labor and the responsibility which the war imposed, he had trusted to his Secretary, when not in conflict with his own opinions, as he had trusted other Secretaries. The currency and national finances had not, in the tumult of hostilities, been specialties with him. When Mr. Chase, who was understood to be a constitutional hard-money man, yielded to the opposite doctrine, assented to the issue of irredeemable paper currency, legalizing it as money, making paper during war a lawful tender for debt, and connected with this policy the establishment of national banks, the President had acquiesced in the proceedings, though some of the Cabinet had questioned their wisdom and correctness. Governor Tod of Ohio, who was first offered the Treasury on the retirement of Mr. Chase, was a Democrat in his antecedents, a resolute supporter of the war for the Union, and the Administration in its measures, but was opposed to an irredeemable paper currency; was an avowed hard-money man of the Jackson and Benton school; consequently not a disciple of Mr. Chase, nor an admirer of his financial policy, though in the emergency created by the war he acquiesced and did not oppose it. Mr. Fessenden, a Whig of the old school, was the opposite of Governor Tod on banking and paper-money questions, past and present. It was a mystery not easily susceptible of explanation—certainly not very consistent—that two men of such opposing views on currency, money, and finance should have been successively and within a few days invited to the same important position. The result proved that the President, if committed to no financial policy, had acted with political shrewdness in the steps which he had taken. The appointments were made without consultation or advice with his Cabinet. In tendering the office to Governor Tod, an old Jacksonian Democrat, he disarmed, in a measure, or blunted, the edge of Democratic hostility. It did not disappoint him that Tod declined to step into the shoes which Mr. Chase vacated. Perhaps he would have been disappointed had he accepted. It would have been difficult, in the then existing state of things, to change the financial policy of the Government; and Governor Tod—an Ohio man as well as Mr. Chase—could not, with his convictions, if he possessed the requisite talents and ability, adopt it. On the other hand, when the President called upon Mr. Fessenden, he invited to his council the right hand man of Mr. Chase—the chairman of the finance committee of the Senate, the participant in and adviser of all the Treasury measures which had been adopted throughout Mr. Chase's administration of the department. It was difficult for the friends of that gentleman to take exceptions or umbrage to the appointment, or to condemn the financial management of his most conspicuous adviser and confidant. By the two selections thus made it was apparent the President was wedded to none of the disputed financial theories or systems.

The policy of the Treasury which had been instituted was not changed with the change of the Secretary; and the Administration lost no strength in consequence, but was really benefited, for Mr. Fessenden, if he had less executive power and ability than Mr. Chase, had incurred no enmities, was opposed by no rivalries, but enjoyed the general confidence of the country.

If Mr. Chase experienced disappointment from the course which things had taken, and in which most of his considerate partisans acquiesced, he and they had the good sense to submit to what they could not control, though there were occasional expressions in private of uneasy discontent. The President well understood the case, and had little apprehension from that quarter. Few persons could better feel the public pulse or judge more correctly the sentiments and wishes of the people, their views on important questions, and their estimate, whether right or wrong, of men. The course of events had satisfied him that Mr. Chase, whatever might be his mental strength, did not possess that inspiring magnetism which controls or leads the popular mind, nor had he the political power which derives strength from public opinion. He had courted the radicals and possessed such standing and influence that they would have consented as an alternative to make him their candidate, but he was not in all respects what they demanded in a leader. He declined to commit himself fully to their ultra views, and when they became convinced he had not the popular support which they once supposed he possessed, he was no longer their man. He had assented to the amnesty proclamation, was less a centralist and more of a constitutionalist than the radical managers required, had regard for the rights of the States—rights which it was the object of Stevens, Davis, and others to break down. They therefore felt little reluctance in abandoning him. Nor was Fremont, who had been substituted at Cleveland, a favorite with them. His letter of acceptance, while it showed he was as emphatic in his hostility to Lincoln as they could wish, was in other respects exceptionable. Thaddeus Stevens, skilful beyond others as a party tactician, shrewd, cunning, audacious, and unscrupulous, had never been an admirer of Fremont, and became indifferent after the Cleveland nomination in regard to candidates. The great ends which

he labored to attain were subjugation of the Southern poeple, confiscation of their property, reduction of their States to provinces,
and national centralization; but these ends were no nearer consummation with Fremont than with Lincoln.

The Winter Davis reconstruction act, as it was called, which
from the time of its introduction, in February, had been used
as an instrument to shape the course of the Republican party in
the selection of a candidate and also to influence the action of
the President, had lingered through the session until after the
convention at Baltimore renominated Mr. Lincoln—a result that
was accomplished despite the chicanery of the managing radicals. Not succeeding in defeating his nomination, they persisted
in pressing the law that was designed to override his amnesty
proclamation and reconstruction policy, which they pronounced
Executive assumptions. It was claimed that the President must
not act on these important questions until "after obtaining the
assent of Congress"; that "the Executive ought not to be permitted to handle this great question"; that "it belongs to the
Senate and the House of Representatives." It was asked in reply
if the right of the President to pardon, grant amnesty, and prescribe a method of reconstruction was denied, that the friends
of the bill should point out the provision in the Constitution
which authorized Congress to exercise any more power than the
President. It was of course impossible for the radicals to give any
satisfactory answer, and they fell back on the phrase that Congress shall guarantee to every State a republican form of government, which is no grant of power to Congress to pardon, to grant
amnesty, to make new constitutions for the States or destroy the
old ones.

Congress adjourned on the Fourth of July, and the passage
of the bill had been delayed until the last hour of the session;
consequently the bill did not reach the President in time for him
to assign the reasons why he was unprepared to give it his approval. Not doubting that it would become a law, the gentlemen who had prepared and navigated the bill, with its various
proposed amendments, and directed the discussion which at op-
portune times had taken place, congratulated themselves on the
consummation of their labors as a crowning radical achievement

at the moment of separation. The same gentlemen were astounded and indignant a few days later on reading the proclamation of the President on the 8th of July informing the country that Congress had passed a bill which expressed the sense of
that department of the Government for restoring the States in
rebellion to their proper practical relation in the Union, which
plan it was thought fit to lay before the people for their consideration, as the Executive department had already done in the
amnesty proclamation and annual message of December. Thus
presenting the case, he said:

> Now, therefore, I, Abraham Lincoln, President of the
> United States, do proclaim, declare, and make known, that
> while I am, as I was in December last, when by proclama-
> tion I propounded a plan for restoration, unprepared by
> a formal approval of this bill to be inflexibly committed to
> any single plan of restoration, and while I am also unpre-
> pared to declare that the free State constitutions and govern-
> ments already adopted and installed in Arkansas and Lou-
> isiana shall be set aside and held for naught, thereby re-
> pelling and discouraging the loyal citizens who have set up
> the same, as to further effort, or to declare a constitutional
> competency in Congress to abolish slavery in the States, but
> at the same time sincerely hoping and expecting that a con-
> stitutional amendment abolishing throughout the nation
> may be adopted, nevertheless I am fully satisfied with the
> system for restoration contained in the bill as one very
> proper for the loyal people of any State choosing to adopt
> it; and that I am, and at all times shall be, prepared to give
> the Executive aid and assistance to any such people, so soon
> as military resistance to the United States shall have been
> suppressed in any such State, and the people thereof shall
> have sufficiently returned to their obedience to the Consti-
> tution and the laws of the United States, in which case
> military governors will be appointed with directions to pro-
> ceed according to the bill.

This presentation of the issue or difference between the
the President and the radical schemers in Congress, involving

the distinctive and fundamental principles of each, was so plain and truthful that it could not be denied, and yet it placed the radicals in such a predicament that they could not afford to be nor were they disposed to be silent. A very elaborate manifesto, or as it was termed a protest, was therefore prepared against the President and his proclamation, which was signed by Senator Wade and H. Winter Davis of the House of Representatives, who had been chairmen of the committees of their respective houses in reporting and carrying through the Congressional reconstruction law to which the President did not give his approval. This manifesto or protest arraigning President Lincoln was addressed "to the supporters of the Government," and began by saying:

> We have read without surprise but not without indignation, the proclamation of the President of the 8th of July, 1864.
> The supporters of the Administration are responsible to the country for its conduct, and it is their right and duty to check the encroachments of the Executive on the authority of Congress, and to require it to confine itself to its proper sphere.
> It is impossible to pass in silence this proclamation without neglecting that duty; and having as much responsibility as any others in supporting the Administration, we are not disposed to fail in the other duty of asserting the rights of Congress.

The protest, illogical, unconstitutional in its premises, filled with technicalities, assumptions, misstatements, and misrepresentations which extended through several pages, too long to be quoted here, charges the President with equivocation and falsehood, and proceeds, among other things, to say:

> The proclamation is neither an approval nor a veto of the bill; it is therefore a document unknown to the laws and Constitution of the United States.
> So far as it contains an apology for not signing the bill

it is a political manifesto against the friends of the Government.

So far as it proposes to execute the bill which is not a law it is a grave Executive usurpation.

It is fitting that the facts necessary to enable the friends of the Administration to appreciate the apology and the usurpation be spread before them.

Alluding to that part of the proclamation where the President says it is fit the Congressional as well as the Executive plan of reconstruction should be presented to the people, the protest asks:

By what authority of the Constitution? In what forms? The result to be declared by whom? With what effect when ascertained.

Insinuating that the President has a purpose in his leniency and tolerance toward the rebels, Messrs. Wade and Davis say:

The President by preventing this bill from becoming a law holds the electoral votes of the rebel States at *the dictation of his personal ambition.*

If those votes turn the balance in his favor, is it to be supposed that his competitor, defeated by such means, will acquiesce?

If the rebel majority assert their supremacy in those states, and send votes which elect an enemy of the Government, will we not repel his claims?

And is not that civil war for the Presidency inaugurated by the votes of the rebel States?

Seriously impressed with these dangers, Congress, "the proper constitutional authority," formally declared that there are no State governments in the rebel States, and provided for their erection at a proper time.

The protest goes on to say:

Under the Constitution, the right to Senators and Representatives is inseparable from a State government.

If there be a State government, the right is absolute.

If there be no State government, there can be no Senators or Representatives chosen.

The two Houses of Congress are expressly declared to be the sole judges of their own members.

When, therefore, Senators and Representatives are admitted, the State government under whose authority they were chosen is conclusively established; when they are rejected, its existence is as conclusively rejected and denied; and to this judgment the President is bound to submit.

The President proceeds to express his unwillingness "to declare a constitutional competency in Congress to abolish slavery in States" as another reason for not signing the bill.

But the bill nowhere proposes to abolish slavery in States.

The bill did provide that all *slaves* in the rebel States should be *manumitted*.

And as regards the proclamation itself:

A more studied outrage upon the legislative authority of the people has never been perpetrated.

Passing a multitude of captious and denunciatory flings at the President and his policy, the radical protest concludes with the following admonition to the Chief Magistrate:

The President has greatly presumed on the forbearance which the supporters of his Administration have so long practised, in view of the arduous conflict in which we are engaged and the reckless ferocity of our political opponents.

But he must understand that our support is of a cause and not of a man; that the authority of Congress is paramount and must be respected: that the whole body of the Union men of Congress will not submit to be impeached by him of rash and unconstitutional legislation; and if he wishes our support, *he must confine himself to his Executive* duties: to *obey and execute,* not make the laws; to suppress by arms armed rebellion, and *leave political reorganization to Congress.*

If the supporters of the Government fail to insist on this, they become responsible for the usurpations which they fail to rebuke, and are justly liable to the indignation of the

people, whose rights and security, committed to their keeping, they sacrifice.

Let them consider the remedy of these usurpations, and
having found it, fearlessly execute it.

B. F. WADE,
Chairman Senate Committee.
H. WINTER DAVIS,
Chairman Committee House of Representatives on the Re-
bellious States.

This radical, factious, party appeal "to the supporters of the
Government" from the official organs of a majority in Congress,
at a crisis when the Administration was putting forth its entire
energies to sustain the Government, published at the commencement of a political campaign for the choice of Chief Magistrate,
had obviously other objects in view than that of strengthening
the President in his efforts to suppress the rebellion. The missile
was aimed at Abraham Lincoln by ostensible friends, but who
had for months labored to supersede him and defeat his policy
of amnesty and reconstruction. The two gentlemen whose names
were appended and who with the assistance and counsel of
others prepared the protest, were the representative men of a
clique in Congress who by caucus machinery and party discipline
controlled the majority of that body. Had Congress been in
session when the President's proclamation was published, the
same machinery and the same discipline might have had some
effect. As it was, Congress having adjourned and the members
separated and at their homes, where their thoughts and reflec-
tions had free exercise, the protest was little regarded by them
and met with no favorable response from the country. Nevertheless the manifesto from two among the most conspicuous leaders of the Union party in Congress had, with an accumulation of
troubles and cares in the summer of 1864, a depressing effect on
the President.

Military successes were at a stand, and did not come up to
public expectation. General Grant had promised the President
personally, in presence of the Cabinet, that he would capture
Richmond if furnished with a sufficient number of troops, which

he was assured he should have, and the power of the nation had
been taxed to fulfil that assurance. The vast army of the Potomac
for a time made advances toward Richmond; but the waste and
slaughter, the immense sacrifices of blood and treasure to sustain
the General and reinforce the army so that its numbers should
not diminish, drew heavily on the Government and country. It
was said by General Grant at the commencement of his march
toward Richmond that he should continue on that line if it
took him all summer. The Administration and country ap-
plauded his pluck and persistency, and responded with unstinted
offerings of men and means to his calls for support after the
successive terrible losses at the Wilderness, Spottsylvania, Cold
Harbor, and almost every step, indeed, of that bloody march.
Whatever losses were sustained were immediately repaired by
reinforcements, so that the progress of the troops was still onward; but these vast efforts were exhausting to the country and
severely trying to the Administration, which was held responsible for all the disasters that occurred, but received little credit
for any military successes. The great army of Grant, after immense slaughter, though it did not retreat, because constantly
strengthened, had, without other results than the loss of more
men than the entire army of Lee and at a cost of hundreds of
millions of treasure, reached the position near Richmond from
which McClellan had been withdrawn in 1862. There it remained for months inactive, and its immobility caused great
discontent through the North and West. The President had supplied the army with additional troops, so that Grant had a
greater command on the James than when he left the Potomac;
but the President, while he sent him men could not furnish his
general with tact and strategy to capture the capital of the Confederacy. He had an army twice the number of that of Lee, but
seemed incapable of accomplishing anything—lay inert and
almost passive, at an expense of more than a million per day,
on the banks of the James, not only during the summer of 1864,
but until after the fall of Fort Fisher and the advance of Sherman
in the spring of 1865.

The failure of Grant to take Richmond, after his bloody

overland march and the great sacrifices which had been made to reach it, was discouraging.

The President, borne down with the anxiety and labor of recruiting, reinforcing, and supplying the army, which was doing so little, in inspiring the country, disappointed in its expectations of military success, in warding off the blows of radical friends, and in reconciling political differences among his supporters, many of whom were opposing instead of strengthening and supporting his measures, began to feel that the Democrats would be likely to succeed in the political campaign that was then progressing.

Entering his office on one of these days, when it was evident that McClellan was to be nominated by the Democrats, when reverses prevailed, when affairs were dark, and many friends on whom he felt the Government ought to be enabled to rely were desponding—some of them, like Greeley, proposing impracticable schemes, and not very creditable terms for peace, and others were complaining because a more unrelenting course was not pursued—when the Democrats were assailing him for arbitrary measures, and both Democrats and radicals were accusing him of usurpations and holding him, not the military commander, accountable for our slaughtered countrymen and slow progress in suppressing the rebellion, he handed me a sealed envelope with a request that I would write my name across the back of it. One or two members of the Cabinet had already done so. In handing it to me he remarked that he would not then inform me of the contents of the paper enclosed, had no explanation to make, but that he had a purpose, and at some future day I should be informed of it, and be present when the seal was broken. Some three months later, after the election had terminated, all the Cabinet being present, he brought out this sealed document, which he opened and read. It was as follows:

EXECUTIVE MANSION, ⎫
WASHINGTON, AUGUST 23, 1864. ⎭

This morning, as for some days past, it seems exceedingly probable that this Administration will not be reëlected. Then it will be my duty to coöperate with the President elect

so as to save the Union between the election and the inauguration, as he will have secured his election on such grounds
that he cannot possibly save it afterward.

A. LINCOLN.

Mr. Lincoln had, after his election in 1860, and preceding his
inauguaration in 1861, when the great secession storm which
threatened the Union was impending, and States and sections
were organized to resist the Government, received no word of
encouragement, no friendly counsel, no generous support from
the retiring administration. He felt that neglect of himself and
the apparent disregard of the public welfare, and, remembering
it, he was determined that General McClellan, who, from the
then indications, would be nominated and elected, should, in
that event, receive his willing assistance and that of the Administration to preserve the Union, though chosen by men who opposed him and his efforts in the national cause.

8

The Opposition to Lincoln in 1864

In this essay, written shortly before his death and published posthumously, Welles returns to the theme of the election of 1864. Again he reviews the efforts of the radicals to displace the President, and he absolves Lincoln of all blame for what he conceives to be the mismanagement of Grant's 1864 campaign before Richmond.

THE FIRST SESSION of the thirty-eighth Congress closed on the 4th of July, 1864. It was the year of a presidential election, and a perverse and discontented spirit manifested itself throughout the session. Besides the open opposition of democrats, the radical element was dissatisfied with the president's policy of conciliation, amnesty, and reconstruction, enunciated in the annual message and amnesty proclamation of the 8th of December, 1863, at the commencement of the session. The democrats were in sympathy with the rebels, and opposed to the war measures of the administration and to the war itself. The radicals opposed the renomination and reëlection of President Lincoln, and those measures of the administration which tended to reconciliation and the reëstablishment of the Union on the basis of the equality of political rights of the States, such as existed prior to the war of secession. With these extremists the general government had ceased to be conventional; was not a federation of States with derivative and limited powers, formed by and with the consent of the States, but was central and imperial, possessing original, inherent, unlimited, and absolute authority over

Atlantic Monthly, XLI (March, 1878).

persons, as well as States, throughout the republic. This combination or faction denied the political equality and refused to recognize any reserved sovereignty of the States; ignored the fact that the federal government had been created, by these local sovereignties which had established it, by a written constitution, specifying and defining the powers with which the general government is invested and expressly forbidding the exercise of any powers not granted or incident thereto; claimed that Congress had supreme power, and was an autocracy or legislative despotism with, if it chose to exercise it, authority over States and people in their social and political relations. Emancipation by the president as commander-in-chief of the military and naval forces was not sufficient without congressional assent. It was denounced as an executive assumption, and legislative action was necessary for its consummation.

War had intensified the antislavery feeling, and zeal for the slave and the emancipated colored people so kindled emotional enthusiasm as to make the radicals oblivious of law and the legal and constitutional rights of the whites. Under the new dispensation brought about by the rebellion, it was insisted that Congress could overrule the States, which, in the formation of the federal government, had reserved to themselves control over persons in their respective limits, and claimed that the general government could decree by federal power the equality of blacks and whites, place the ignorant on a par with the intelligent, regulate by law their social and political intercourse, and bestow upon the stolid, uneducated, and incapable negroes the privilege of voting in the elections, and at the same time preclude, without legal trial, the whites who had participated or were implicated in the rebellion.

Mr. Lincoln and all his cabinet, in the first years of the war, opposed these radical innovations; but Mr. Chase ultimately, when he became a competitor for the office of president, gave his approval to negro suffrage, limiting his assent, however, to such of the colored population as could intelligently exercise the privilege. Very considerable change of opinion—called progress by the radical philanthropists—took place during the war in relation to our governmental system of granted federal powers, and the retained local authority and reserved sovereignty of the States. Emotional philanthropy was made to supersede statutory and constitutional law. Rights of persons and rights of property, which the States had refused to concede to the general government— rights which belonged to and were under the control of the respective commonwealths,—began to be disregarded by the radicals, who were constantly increasing in numbers as the war progressed. Confusion prevailed in regard to citizenship, inhabitancy, and legal residence in a State, but the whole was generalized and absorbed in central legislative supremacy, under the specious and popular expression of "the equality of all men before the law"; an expression more taking in consequence of the growing hostility against slavery and the arrogance of the slave owners, who had plunged the country into civil war.

At no time had Mr. Lincoln been more depressed than when, in 1864, he wrote his desponding note of the 23d of August, stating that the democrats, in his opinion, would be successful in the approaching election. An accumulation of disheartening difficulties, internal and external in the free States—differences such as loyal and disloyal, democrat and republican, republican and radical, personal and sectional—had clouded the administration during the spring and summer, with scarcely a cheering ray to lighten or encourage the government in the mighty struggle to suppress the rebellion. Whilst putting forth the utmost energies of the nation to maintain the Union, which for three years the rebels had, with immense armies, striven to dissolve, the president, from the day of his inauguration, encountered in the free States the steady opposition of the broken, but yet powerfully organized democratic party, which had been in political sympathy with the rebels prior to his election, and which still affiliated with its old party associates.

Added to these, and quite as discouraging and more disheartening than either during the year 1864, were the embarrassing intrigues of discontented and aspiring factions among republicans, growing out of the approaching presidential election and the radical claim for legislative supremacy in the conduct of the government. The opportunity was seized, not only by personal aspirants, but by the disaffected of every description, who, although disagreeing among themselves, had the common purpose, which they exercised, of weakening the president in the public estimation, creating a distrust of his capacity, and impairing confidence in his administration. His ability and energy in prosecuting the war were questioned, his conciliatory policy towards the rebels and his disinclination to confiscate their property were denounced, and his amnesty and reconstruction measures were censured and condemned. The expediency of a change in the presidential office for a more resolute and arbitrary executive was urged by radical congressional leaders during the whole of the first session of the thirty-eighth Congress, and opposition to the president was continued after its adjournment.

The *fiasco* at Cleveland in May had not entirely extinguished the visionary dreams of aspirants and their friends, who still entertained lingering hopes that adverse affairs, or some adventitious circumstance, might induce a compromise which would withdraw both Lincoln and Fremont and result in the selection of a new candidate. The malevolence of extremists, who were bent on vengeance against the rebels and their subjugation, the confiscation of their property, the overthrow of their old established local government, the reduction of their States to provinces, and the creation of new governments for them under congressional dictation, was active and determined.

The new secretary of the treasury, who took his seat in the cabinet on the 5th of July, was dismayed and appalled, at the commencement of his executive duties, by the overwhelming calls for means to carry on the war. Neither the resources nor the credit of the country could, in his apprehension, meet the demands that were made, and he did not conceal from the president his anxiety and fears. His predecessor, after his retirement on the 30th of June, did not participate in the political party conflicts that agitated the country, and manifested no interest nor rendered any efficient support to the president in the pending political contest. Not until after the failure of the scheme to induce or compel the president and Fremont to decline, nor until after the meeting of the democratic convention at Chicago and the nomination of General McClellan, did he appear and take

any active part in political affairs. Under his administration of
the treasury a debt of nearly two thousand millions of dollars
had been incurred, besides an absorption of the entire revenues
received from every source. The condition of the finances on the
accession of Mr. Fessenden was so deplorable that a stouter and
healthier physique and more vigorous mental power than he possessed might have been discouraged by the prospect and requirements.

The substitution of irredeemable paper for money—making
it a legal tender for debts, a policy adopted early in the war—
had so inflated and depreciated the currency as to affect values
and render loans to the government almost ruinous to the
country. At no period of the national existence had the credit
of the government been reduced to so low an ebb as in the
months of July and August following the renomination of Mr.
Lincoln and the retirement of Mr. Chase.

Attending this distressing state of the finances was the
painful inaction of the military, particularly the inert and apparently helpless condition of our lieutenant-general and his
host, who after the sanguinary march of the army of the Potomac from the Rapidan, arrived before Richmond on the
13th of June.

Perhaps too high expectations of immediate results were
entertained by the administration and the country; but days
and weeks dragged on with no improvement; hope deferred
made the heart sick; the president, not the general, was held
accountable by the country for delay; designing partisans imputed non-action of the military to the president's conciliatory
policy, which it was claimed, encouraged the rebels and impaired
the efficiency of our troops.

While Grant, with his immense force, threatened Richmond,
Lee, with greatly inferior numbers, protected the rebel capital,
and fertile in strategy and resources, checked and distracted
the lieutenant-general, who had perseverance and obstinacy, and
but little else. On these the president was obliged to rely,
amidst censure and denunciation from the radicals, until events
might favor the Union arms. The raid of Early down the
Shenandoah in July, and his advance upon Washington, which,

stripped of troops to recruit Grant, was in an unprotected state and might have been captured; the demonstration by the rebels upon Baltimore and the seizure of the great Northern railroads, —burning their bridges and capturing trains; the taking and setting fire to Chambersburg, carrying terror through Pennsylvania and alarming other States, were trying to the administration. Military failures and inactivity everywhere rendered the summer gloomy and disheartening. The president, while disappointed by the immobility of the army, and exerting himself to inspire the country with hope, was himself assailed with bitterness by radical chiefs who should have been his champions and supporters, and his administration and measures were unsparingly denounced by a reckless combination that condemned his policy.

The feuds of the republicans, which were in active operation in 1864, gave great encouragement to the peace democrats, who were perfecting a vigorous party organization for the presidential election. They were well aware, long before the Wade and Winter Davis protest, of the hostility of the radicals to Mr. Lincoln, to his amnesty proclamation and his reconstruction views, and of the determination to defeat him and his conciliatory policy. His amicable policy the democrats did not dislike, but to obtain party ascendency and possession of the government, they were as zealous as the radicals to prevent his reëlection.

The party and personal intrigues of secessionists, democrats, and radicals through the summer, to impair confidence in the president and overthrow the administration that was spending its strength to suppress the rebellion and preserve the national integrity, seemed a sad commentary on the patriotism of the people and the working of our political system. No small portion of the leading offical minds of the country, and particularly of Congress, was involved in these intrigues against the executive struggling with reverses and with impending peril to maintain the Union and the national existence. Much has been justly written and published of what was done by the gallant officers in the field and on the waves, but comparatively little is recorded of the trials and responsibilities of those who were entrusted with the government, and especially the president, in those unhappy days. Besides encountering rebels in open, armed resistance to the government, and providing men and supplies for the forces in active service, he and his associates were compelled to meet the opposition of professed friends, on whom they felt they ought to have been enabled to rely for support, and to meet political and party assaults, secretly and openly at work for their overthrow.

The Cleveland convention, elaborately got up in May, proved a fiasco, and the Baltimore convention in June, which the discontented and mischievous elements had exerted themselves to postpone or control, had renominated Mr. Lincoln. The secretary of the treasury, around whom the extremists had through the winter and spring prepared to rally, resigned a few days after Mr. Lincoln's renomination.

Still persistent in their sectional and hostile intentions, the radicals and the malcontents entertained an indefinite but vague hope that they might, near the close of the political campaign, compel the withdrawal of both the president and Fremont and the substitution of another name, and thus unite all republicans on a more radical candidate. There was with some a lingering idea, rather than expectation, that the democratic convention, which had been postponed from the 4th of July to the 29th of August, might think it expedient to select the ex-secretary of the treasury for their candidate. Mr. Chase remarks in his diary, on the 6th of July, that Pomeroy informed him that democratic senators had said that now the secretary was out of the administration, "We'll go with you now for Chase." This, says the ex-secretary "meant nothing but a vehement desire to overthrow the existing administration, but might mean much if the democrats would only cut loose from slavery and go for freedom and the protection of labor by a national currency. *If they would do that, I would cheerfully go for any man they might nominate.*" But as time progressed, and the drafts and calls for troops multiplied, and non-action and military reverses prevailed, this remote thought that the democrats might nominate Mr. Chase proved delusive; for the democrats, encouraged by republican dissen-

sions and national disaster, began to entertain a confident expectation that they might be successful with a candidate who
had been earlier relieved and for different reasons.

By midsummer it was apparent, beyond a reasonable doubt,
that the democrats would, at Chicago, make General McClellan
their standard-bearer. When this became evident, a last earnest
effort was made by the radical extremists against Lincoln, but
the result proved futile. The scheme or design to induce or
compel both him and Fremont to withdraw, in order to substitute a candidate more revolutionary and acceptable to themselves,
was put in operation by the radicals. The nomination of Fremont, when made, was a ruse of the master spirits, intended by
them to terminate in the retirement of both Fremont and
Lincoln. It was neither a wise nor profound expedient in its
inception, and the expanding hopes and vigorous efforts of the
democrats, who began to believe in their own success, dwarfed
the intrigue. In August, when the radical demonstrations for a
compromise candidate were to be made, the prospect was not
promising; the chief movers held aloof, and subordinates were
pushed forward to issue calls in several quarters, intended as
feelers of the public pulse. The most marked and significant
of these calls was in Boston, where several gentlemen, known
agitators, men of some intellectual capacity, persistent abolitionists, independent of party though lately acting with the
republicans, but really of very little political influence, theoretical in their views and fanatical in their prosecution, ardent
admirers of Senator Sumner, with whom they acted and who
acted with them, came to the front in the scheme to get rid of
Mr. Lincoln.

The president, these "independents" were aware, did not
recognize the negroes as entitled by law, or by the government
as constituted, to the same social and political privileges as the
whites; nor as possessed of the capacity, certainly not the culture,
to exercise those privileges intelligently, were the federal government instead of the States empowered to act upon such subjects.

These political theorists were not reluctant to go forward
in a last attempt to set aside the Cleveland and Baltimore nomin-

ations by making use of the Cleveland nominee to effect it. The
letter of the Boston gentlemen to Fremont displays the animus
and intent of the discontented against Mr. Lincoln.

BOSTON, *August* 21, 1864.

GENERAL FREMONT:

Sir, — you must be aware of the wide and growing dissatisfaction in the republican ranks with the presidential nomination at Baltimore; and you may have seen notices of a
movement, just commenced, to unite the thorough and
earnest friends of a rigorous prosecution of the war in a new
convention, which shall represent the patriotism of all
parties.

To facilitate that movement it is emphatically advisable
that the candidates nominated at Cleveland and Baltimore
should withdraw, and leave the field entirely free for such a
united effort.

Permit us, sir, to ask whether, in case Mr. Lincoln will
withdraw, you will do so, and join your fellow-citizens in
this attempt to place the administration on a basis broad as
the patriotism of the country and as its needs.

GEORGE L. STEARNS   ELIZUR WRIGHT
S. R. URINO   EDWARD HABICH
JAMES M. STONE   SAMUEL G. HOWE

This movement, emanating from hitherto pronounced friends,
at a period of general depression, affected the president more
than the direct assaults of the radicals in Congress. The finances
were at that time low and the resources of the country apparently
exhausted; the calls for men and means were enormous; the draft
was opposed, and capitalists were reluctant to invest in government securities; military operations were at a stand-still; a political presidential campaign, involving every variety of issue,
was in progress; the great inimical political party, striving for a
change of administration, was animated, vigorous, and active,
when this untoward intrigue to compel the chief magistrate to
relinquish a longer official connection with the government was
begun. It was an ungenerous and unfriendly request; a blow from
a portion of his friends, who sought success by antagonizing him,

the national executive, who was discharging the duties of chief
magistrate and had the confidence of the country, with one who
had neither personal nor political strength,—a request that he
would put himself and the whole republican party of the country
on a level with the factious gathering at Cleveland, and decline
being a candidate. The proposition, presumptious and absurd,
which as he and the leading minds of the administration believed,
and as events proved, was made by friends of Sumner and
Chase, and probably made honestly by those whose names were
appended, struck the president painfully. It was made, as will be
observed, on the 21st of August. On the 23d the president wrote
the desponding note to which I have already referred, stating that
the probabilities were that "this administration will not be re-
elected." He misjudged, for the demonstration was factious and
feeble; the good sense of the people was against it, and did not
respond to it.

The protest of the congressional radicals, through Wade and
Winter Davis, against the amnesty and reconstruction proclamation had inspired the democrats, who were organizing for their
national convention, shrewdly postponed from the 4th of July to
the 29th of August; and the proposition to "swap horses when
crossing the river"—in other words to change candidates at such
a crisis of the presidential campaign—had impressed them, as it
did the president, with an idea that they would be triumphant
in the approaching election. They had also taken encouragement
from the tardy and inefficient operations of the Union armies,—
particularly from the immobility of the immense force under
Grant, of whom there had been high, perhaps unreasonable expectations, from the day he took his departure from the Rapidan
in May, but who had really accomplished nothing except a sanguinary march to the vicinity of Richmond. The democrats had
never been impressed with the genius, strategic skill, or military
capacity of the lieutenant-general, but always placed a lower
estimate than the republicans on his qualities as a commander;
the bloody march, with its inconsequential results, had not
changed but confirmed this opinion. That march had been
accomplished: he reoccupied the ground from which McClellan
was withdrawn, but at such a sacrifice that the grief of the country

and the wailing of almost every household for its fallen heroes counter-balanced whatever joy was felt for an achievement so dearly effected. At the same time the sacrifice strengthened the democrats, who were organizing for their national convention on the basis of peace and of an abandonment of hostilities by the government.

It was believed that Richmond would be speedily captured by the armies, to reinforce which the energies and resources of the country had been severely taxed. The whole collected forces of the armies of the Potomac and the James were at the disposal of Grant, who, under the president, had been made general-in-chief of the armies of the United States. The country was impatient of delay; it had anticipated certain success, and the belief in speedy, triumphant results was fostered by the administration. The secretary of war, to appease public expectation, published, for a time, daily bulletins, addressed to General Dix, that the army movements were onward.

The garrisons had been stripped of troops to keep the armies in full force; yet nothing had been accomplished after reaching the James, from whence McClellan had been recalled, except the sacrifice of nearly one half of the army. General Grant possessed great tenacity and persistency,—high qualities in a commander,—which enabled him to hold on to what he had in hand, and to press forward so long as he was reinforced and sustained by the administration; but unfortunately he was endowed with no genius, with little strategic skill, nor had he power to originate plans and devise measures to overcome his skillful and able antagonist. He reached the banks of the James, and he remained there, accomplishing nothing further, while the country was daily expecting to hear of the fall of Richmond. The president, and not the general, was held responsible for this procrastination: he was denounced for inefficiency and usurpation by the radicals, and accused of inability to conquer a peace by the democrats.

The wounded soldiers sent to Washington to be nursed were living witnesses of the country's agony. Miles of hospital barracks were erected in Washington, and filled with thousands upon thousands of brave men, maimed and dying. This almost innumerable host, from among the noblest heroes and most patriotic spirits of the land, who had periled their lives and poured forth their blood for their country, was, during that sad summer, an affecting spectacle that grieved the hearts of all, and of none more than the president, who was blamed and held responsible for the killed and wounded by a large portion of his countrymen. Such of the mutilated soldiers as could get from their beds were accustomed to cheer and give glad utterance to their feelings as the president with his escort daily passed between his summer residence at the Soldier's Home and the Executive Mansion. The always welcome voices of these brave and suffering men touched him tenderly, and were in strong contrast with the mischievous radical element which, amidst his tiring and exhaustive labors for the Union, was intriguing against him. While these gallant men who sympathized with the president lay suffering for their love of country and devotion to the Union, factious party intriguers were employing their time and talents in denunciatory complaints of his management, and in urging an unconstitutional and unjust sectional exclusion of one third of the States from the Union.

General Richard Taylor has recently stated in the North American Review: "After the battle of Chickamauga, in 1863, General Grant was promoted to the command of the armies of the United States, and called to Washington. In a conference at the war office, between him, President Lincoln, and Secretary Stanton, the approaching campaign in Virginia was discussed. Grant said the advance on Richmond should be made by the James River. It was replied that government required the interposition of an army between Lee and Washington, and would not consent, at that late day, to the adoption of a plan that would be taken by the public as a confession of previous error. Grant observed he was indifferent as to routes, but if the government preferred its own—so often tried—to the one he suggested, it must be prepared for the additional loss of one hundred thousand men. The men were promised; Grant accepted the governmental plan of campaign, and was supported to the end. The above came to me well authenticated, and I have no doubt of its correctness."

There is no reason to doubt the veracity of General Taylor,

who says this statement came to him "well authenticated;" but those who knew the three persons said to have had "a conference at the war office," when General Grant came to Washington to receive the commission of lieutenant-general, will question the accuracy of the statement. It is now made public that General Grant had prescience of his reverses and losses if he took the Rapidan route, for the first time, nearly fourteen years after the event took place, when two of the three persons named are in their graves. While they, or either of the two, were alive, there was no claim of this sort set up to relieve the survivor and principal actor; no attempt to cast upon those now dead the responsibility of the bloody march to Richmond, which they are said to have insisted upon in opposition to the opinion and judgment of the lieutenant-general, whose duty it was to designate the route, and who did so: that officer had just been promoted for the express purpose of taking command of military operations and the conduct and management of the armies in the approaching campaign. It is known to those intimate with President Lincoln that, while he had usually very decided opinions of his own on military movements, and freely expressed them to his cabinet and at head-quarters, he invariably deferred (yielding what I think was sometimes his better judgment) to the generals in command, for the reason that they were military experts, professionally educated, and, if fit for their positions, were best qualified to decide upon the true course to pursue. If "Grant said the advance on Richmond should be made by the James River," the president, in this as in other cases, would have withdrawn his own opinion, if favorable to the march, and would not have overruled the recently created active general-in-chief.

It seems that the general himself had no very decided opinions on the subject; General Taylor says, "Grant observed *he was indifferent* as to routes, but if the government preferred its own—so often tried—to the one he suggested, it must be prepared for the additional loss of one hundred thousand men." Such a statement would of itself have controlled the president, whose sympathies were great, while Grant was of an unsympathetic nature, and "indifferent" which route he took. President Lincoln was always keenly sensitive upon the subject of the lives and sufferings of the soldiers. Such a statement as General Grant is represented to have made would have shocked the compassionate nature of Lincoln, and been with him decisive against an overland march, provided he, and not the lieutenant-general, was to select the route. He would have supported the general in his preference for the James River route from that fact itself, although it seems to have been a matter of indifference to Lieutenant-General Grant.

But is it to be supposed that Grant anticipated in March, when this conference is reported to have taken place, that in battles such as those of the Wilderness he would lose nearly thirty thousand men, at Spottsylvania ten thousand, and an aggregate which in numbers equaled the entire rebel army under Lee? Before the days of that sanguinary march, over which the whole country became frantic by reason of the slaughtered heroes who poured forth their blood for the Union, the general-in-chief is said to have known of the sacrifice to be made, was indifferent to consequences, and assented, against his convictions, to the bloody route.

But time has elapsed, and history is recording the terrible and apparently unnecessary waste of life; the general begins to feel his responsibility for the immolation, and an attempt is now made to relieve him and impose the responsibility upon others. As well and as truly say Sherman's march through Georgia and the Carolinas, which was attended with no such sacrifice, was an administration measure.

General Grant's first visit to Washington was in March, 1864. It was to receive the commission of lieutenant-general,—an office created with reluctance, and to which he had been promoted through the active exertions of Mr. E. B. Washburne, who represented the Galena district in Congress, and whose zeal in that regard was subsequently rewarded by his appointment as secretary of State, immediately after Grant's inauguration, and his transference after ten days to the French Mission.

This visit of Grant, in March, 1864, to receive honors and full command was very brief. He arrived in Washington on the evening of Tuesday, the 8th of March, and came between nine and ten o'clock to the Executive Mansion. There was on that evening a public and very crowded presidential reception. It was there that Grant was first introduced to President Lincoln. On the following day, Wednesday the 9th, the president and cabinet were specially convened for the ceremony of presenting the commission. At one o'clock, the lieutenant-general entered the council chamber, accompanied by his staff and by Secretary Stanton and General Halleck, when the president formally delivered the commission, and the general, with a few written remarks, received it. A desultory conversation of half an hour took place. General Grant, after receiving the commission, inquired what special service was expected of him. The president replied that the country wanted him to take Richmond; he said our generals had not been fortunate in their efforts in that direction, and asked if the lieutenant-general could do it. Grant, without hesitation, answered that he could if he had the troops. These the president assured him he should have. This was on the afternoon of the 9th; nothing was then said of the James River or any other route. General Grant proceeded to the headquarters of General Meade and the army of the Potomac, in front, from whence he returned to Washington on the afternoon of Friday the 11th, and came at once, on his arrival, to the council chamber, where the cabinet was in session. He did not remain a great while, spoke of his visit to the army, and said he proposed to take command in person, but would retain General Meade. When about to retire, he remarked to the president that he should leave that afternoon for Nashville, to turn over his late command to General Sherman, but would return in two weeks; having but little time, he would be glad to confer with the secretary of war and General Halleck before he left.

Neither on this nor any other occasion, when I was present, was there any expression of preference for the James River route, nor any opposition to the overland march; no statement that the march from the Rapidan would cost one hundred thousand men. Had there been anything of this kind, something of it would probably have been known to me and others. Had there been a proposition for a different route than that which General Meade had commenced, any preference expressed for the James River route, particularly if, in the estimation of the lieutenant-general, it involved one hundred thousand lives, neither the president nor any members of the government would have approved of it, after such a warning. It is represented, however, that there was warning of such a sacrifice, but it was a matter of "indifference" to General Grant, if the government, from pride of opinion, adhered to the overland march.

General Taylor does not tell from what source the information, now for the first time made public, was derived. To be authentic it must have come from one of the three gentlemen who held the conference in the war department. It could not have been from President Lincoln, for, if I mistake not, he and General Taylor never met. When the president was assassinated, General Taylor was in the rebel service.

There were not such intimate and amicable relations between Secretary Stanton and General Taylor as would have begotten confidence of this nature. There was, in fact, mutual distrust and dislike. When General Taylor came to Washington after the close of the war, there was a movement, in which I was informed he participated, for the removal of Mr. Stanton and the appointment of General Grant to be secretary of war. This change, which finally took place at a later period, was in its inception a matter of concert or of assent on the part of both the generals. But President Johnson, who at first acquiesced, failed at the last moment to consummate the arrangement.

I was not advised of that attempt, nor party to it; knew nothing of it until after its failure; but, to quote the words of General Taylor, this information "came to me well authenticated, and I have no doubt of its correctness."

The knowledge of the conference at the war office, in March, 1864, could therefore have scarcely been obtained from Secretary Stanton. There was, I have no doubt, a conference, at the time and place mentioned, between generals Grant and Halleck and Secretary Stanton, because to my personal knowledge and in my presence General Grant asked such a conference. Of the results I have no recollection, if I ever knew them. They were unquestionably preliminary to Grant's assuming active command.

Stanton and Halleck, with whom Grant had this conference on the 11th of March, are known to have been committed to the

plan of making Washington the base of military operations
against Richmond. Secretaries Chase and Stanton had made the
advance against the rebel capital by the York or James river
an objection to General McClellan, when urging his removal in
1862; but the president, although disappointed in McClellan, did
not act on the representations of the two secretaries who urged
the general's recall. After the seven days' disaster before Richmond, President Lincoln consulted General Scott, then at West
Point, and, with his approval, brought Halleck from Corinth to
supersede McClellan at head-quarters. Halleck, after arriving at
Washington, and assuming the direction of army movements,
adopted the views of Stanton and Chase, and the recall of McClellan from the James then became, not a civil, but a military question for the general commanding the armies. The president,
whatever may have been his opinion as to the two routes, did
not yield to his two secretaries, who were not military men, or
better qualified than himself to decide, but he did defer to General Halleck, and acquiesced in the order to recall the army of
the Potomac from the James. No member of the cabinet, however,
save the two who urged it and were opposed to McClellan, knew
of that order until it was issued.

The change urged by Chase and Stanton, and indorsed by
Halleck, of recalling McClellan and taking up a line of march
upon Richmond, with Washington for the base, did not prove a
success. Pope, Burnside, Hooker, and Meade, each acting under
Halleck, had one after another failed to make an advance, and
the latter general was with the army on the Rapidan when
Grant came to Washington and the conference of Grant, Stanton,
and Halleck took place in the war office. That "Grant said the
advance on Richmond should be made by the James River" is
not improbable, for such would seem to be the common-sense
view of every one, professional or otherwise, save the two secretaries and General Halleck.

A general in command does not usually surrender his plans
and yield what he knows to be right to subordinates, against his
own convictions, without overpowering reasons. General Grant
is an exception, for, destitute of originality, he commonly acted
on the ideas and plans of others. In this instance the lieutenant-

general claims to have abandoned the route which he knew to be best, and, horrible to confess,—for the statement of General Taylor must have come from him,—he gave up the route which he knew to be right, and assented to that which he knew to be wrong, and which involved the awful sacrifice of one hundred thousand men, on the suggestion of persons who had opposed and procured the recall of McClellan. Either route was indifferent to Grant, and he took the worst.

In administering the government, and especially in the conduct of the armies, President Lincoln deferred to the military commanders and the conclusions at head-quarters. Is it credible that on the most important occasion of his administration—the greatest military movement of the war—the president would have departed from his uniform course, and disregarded and overruled the highest military officer in the government, who had just been promoted and was about to take command of the armies of the United States? No one who knew Abraham Lincoln can for a moment believe it. He did not so recklessly discharge his executive duties. Moreover, it is asserted that Grant gave warning that if the James River route was not taken, a loss of life exceeding in numbers the whole rebel army under Lee would be the consequence; yet that route was not taken. While Grant was unsympathetic and indifferent on this subject, President Lincoln's sympathies were great, and such a warning would of itself have controlled him. No man more deeply deplored the loss of human life.

It is, I apprehend, a mistake to say that President Lincoln participated in any such conference as stated, but there was an interview between Grant, Stanton, and Halleck at the war office, on the 11th of March, after Grant had visited General Meade and before he returned to Nashville.

This representation, that President Lincoln preferred the sacrifice of one hundred thousand men to the confession of previous error; that he overruled and directed Grant, just made lieutenant-general for the purpose of taking command and directing all the armies and military movements, is an after-thought to cast from the shoulders of General Grant the responsibility of the "bloody march" and place it upon the kind-hearted president. The whole statement is ungenerous and unjust, and in conflict with the character of both the president and the lieutenant-general.

All the facts and details of current events of the period evince the mistake of General Taylor's statement. General Grant returned from Nashville about the first of April, visited Hampton Roads, arranged for the army of the James to ascend that river, and then joining General Meade he placed himself at the head of the army of the Potomac. How communicative he was to the president may been seen from the following encouraging letter, written on the 30th of April, three days before the army broke camp and took up its line of march towards Richmond:—

EXECUTIVE MANSION, WASHINGTON, ⎫
April 30, 1864.   ⎭

LIEUTENANT - GENERAL GRANT,—Not expecting to see you before the spring campaign opens, I wish to express in this way my entire satisfaction with what you have done up to this time, so far as I understand it. The particulars of your plans, I neither know nor seek to know. You are vigilant and self-reliant, and, pleased with this, I wish not to obtrude any restraints or constraints upon you. While I am very anxious that any great disaster or capture of our men in great numbers shall be avoided, I know that these points are less likely to escape your attention than they would mine. If there be anything wanting which is within my power to give, do not fail to let me know it. And now, with a brave army and a just cause, may God sustain you.

Yours very truly,
A. LINCOLN.

There is nothing dictatorial in this letter: "The particulars of your plans *I neither know nor seek to know,*" "I wish not to obtrude any *restraints* or *constraints* upon you," "I am very anxious that any great *disaster* or *capture of our men* in great numbers shall be avoided," etc.

Can any one believe for a moment that the author of that letter would consent to the additional loss of one hundred thousand men "sooner than the adoption of a plan that would be taken by the public as a confession of previous error"? The whole is a calumny on the humane, self-sacrificing, and lion-hearted Lincoln.

9

Lincoln's Triumph in 1864

In this last essay, Welles discusses the triumph of Abraham Lincoln in 1864 against a background of bickering and obstruction. The most interesting part of this article is Welles' account of the resignation of Secretaries Chase and Blair, the former as a result of his equivocal attitude, and the latter, as Welles correctly surmised, as a peace offering to the radicals. Once again the Secretary of the Navy absolves his chief from all guilt in connection with Grant's great losses and discusses the important role of the navy in the capture of Fort Fisher, the last Confederate stronghold on the Atlantic coast.

IN THE SUMMER OF 1864 vague and indefinite rumors were circulated that peace was attainable, and actually desired by the rebels, but that the administration would not listen to overtures or receive propositions which might lead to an adjustment. Some leading and over-officious persons interested themselves in these matters, which were merely subsidiary aids to the peace democrats, projected by the rebels to divide the republicans and to promote democratic success in the pending election. For a brief period these rumors undoubtedly made an impression unfavorable and unjust, as regarded the president. Horace Greeley, often credulous and always ready to engage in public employment, was entrapped by the most skillfully contrived of these intrigues. He became the willing agent of certain prominent rebels who resorted to Canada, and from thence persuaded him that they were authorized by the rebel government to negotiate

Atlantic Monthly, XLI (April, 1878).

peace, and desired his assistance. They asked for full protection to proceed to Washington to effect that object, and made Greeley the medium to convey to the president their application and purpose.

Greeley, thus applied to, at once entered into the scheme, and forwarded their application, with his indorsement that that while he did "not say a just peace is now attainable, he believed it to be so." The president had no belief in the good faith or sincerity of this proceeding, and little doubted that it was a subtle intrigue; but as it emanated from distinguished rebels, and had the indorsement of one of the most influential editors and politicians of the republican party, he was for a moment embarrassed how to treat it or what course to take. Promptly to reject the application thus made and indorsed would not only subject him to misrepresentation, and bring upon him the assaults of the malevolent, but would lead to a misconception of his own ardent desire for peace by many well-meaning men who, weary of war, earnestly praying that hostilities should cease, wished he might accept this advance and permit such conspicuous rebels as Jacob Thompson, C. C. Clay, and their associates, to visit Washington. The advent of these secession gentlemen would not be private and unheralded, but attended with the pomp and proclaimed character of ambassadors or ministers from the Confederate government to negotiate peace. Its effect would be and was evidently intended to divert attention from a vigorous prosecution of the war, and raise hopes through the North which it was the special object of this commission to defeat. Their errand of peace was obviously auxiliary to the peace democrats, and whether accepted or rejected was to be used against the administration in the presidential election. Mortified that so intelligent and eminent a republican as Mr. Greeley should in his officious desire to be useful lend himself to this intrigue of distinguished persons, who presented no credentials, even from the irresponsible rebel organization, the president deputed Greeley himself to proceed to Niagara, communicate with his rebel correspondents, and ascertain their power to act. As an authority to Greeley and an estoppel to future similar intrigues, the president issued the following:—

EXECUTIVE MANSION, WASHINGTON, ⎫
    July 18, 1864.   ⎭

TO WHOM IT MAY CONCERN: Any proposition which embraces the restoration of peace, the integrity of the whole Union, and the abandonment of slavery, and which comes by and with an authority that can control the armies now at war against the United States, will be received and considered by the executive government of the United States, and will be met by liberal terms on other substantial and collateral points; and the bearer or bearers thereof shall have safe conduct both ways.

ABRAHAM LINCOLN.

These and other schemes, projected by real and professed republicans as well as by avowed opponents, while annoying and discouraging, were skillfully met, warded off, and disposed of by the president, who never failed to prove himself able to cope with his adversaries and to be equal to any emergency. Greeley was surprised and taken aback on receiving his appointment as a *quasi* minister or agent, with authority to meet the ambassadorial trio whose mission he indorsed, and with the assurance that any proposition which embraced the restoration of peace and the integrity of the Union would be received, and the bearers should have safe conduct. The rebel representatives and the peace democrats in the North were as much astonished and disappointed with the comprehensive credentials, which extended not only to them and their mission but to any and all others whom it might concern. It virtually muzzled that species of political party electioneering that was intruding itself into the presidential campaign.

The democratic national convention met at Chicago on the 29th of August, to nominate a candidate for president, and to lay down the programme or platform of political principles which the managers professed to believe best for the country, and by which they and their associates were governed. Until within a few days of the meeting of the convention circumstances had favored them. Scarcely a cheering ray had dawned upon the administration after the renomination of Mr. Lincoln until about the time the democratic delegates convened at Chicago. Except the success of the navy in the destruction of the rebel cruiser Alabama by the Kearsarge in June, and the passage of the forts of Mobile Bay by Farragut in August, there had seemed a pall over the Union cause, and all efforts, civil and military, of the administration. Information of the surrender of Fort Morgan was received on the day the democratic convention assembled. That convention pronounced the war a failure. Not only did rambling party declaimers harangue crowds against the despotic and arbitrary measures of the government, which, they said, was alienating the South, but men of eminence, some of whom had enjoyed public confidence and held high official position, participated in the assaults upon the president, who, while thus attacked, was struggling against reverses and armed resistance to the Union.

Added to these attacks of the peace democrats were the denunciations and various intrigues of the radical element in the republican party, which assailed the president personally, and bitterly attacked his conciliatory policy, accusing him of usurpation in his mode and method of striving for peace, and of inefficiency and neglect in not prosecuting the war with greater severity. The democrats and the radicals did not coalesce, were antagonistic; yet each was hostile to the president and opposed his reëlection, but from opposite causes. Among the members of the Chicago convention were such men as James Guthrie, formerly secretary of the treasury, and Charles A. Wickliffe, once postmaster-general, both of Kentucky, Union men at the beginning of the war, uncompromising, however, against the radicals, but now opposed to President Lincoln. They disapproved the policy of the administration, and especially the emancipation of slaves by a military order of the president. Such an act, changing the social and industrial character of nearly one half of the States, was fundamental; one, as they claimed, above and beyond the executive or legislative authority of the federal government; and it could not be legally effected except by the States interested, or possibly by an amendment of the federal constitution. These original Union men were members of the convention at Chicago, and acted in concert with such violent and denunciatory

anti-Union men as Vallandigham, as well as with the more plau-
sible and timid but scarcely less mischievous members of the
convention who refused to recognize war necessity as a justification for emancipation.

As usual with political conventions or assemblages in periods
of high party excitement, the radical and too often the impulsive and inconsiderate extremists, by their vociferous and inflammatory harangues, carried with them a majority of the members, most of whom had in fact been chosen, not for calm and
deliberate judgment, but for their party zeal and intolerance.

On this occasion extraordinary efforts had been made to
strengthen the weak and timid of the party, to oppose the
government, and to fortify the bold and aggressive by a gathering
at Chicago of rebel emissaries and reckless and violent fac-
tionists outside the convention, known as "copperheads," who
were secretly in sympathy with the secessionists. Rumors that a
conflict was inevitable prevailed. It was stated by Colonel Sweet,
and subsequently affirmed by Holt, the judge-advocate-general,
that there was a plot or conspiracy to improve the opportunity
of the meeting of the democratic convention to arouse and in-
flame the masses and ultimately to free the rebel prisoners, of
whom several thousands were confined in Chicago, at Camp
Douglas, and also at Indianapolis and other places. Price and
his bushwhackers in Missouri were to move in concert with an
extensive secret organization that existed throughout the country
under various names, but generally recognized as the Sons of
Liberty, the Golden Circle, Order of American Knights, etc.
These were to inaugurate an uprising which would, in its ramifi-
cations in the approaching election, be decisive.

For some time the war department and General Grant—
whether wisely or unwisely it is not necessary here to discuss—had
set aside and disregarded the cartel for the exchange of prisoners,
and retained in confinement the rebels captured by our troops.
As a consequence, Union soldiers taken in battle were held in
captivity and shut up in Libby, Andersonville, Salisbury, and
other prisons, where, half-starved and half-clad, their sufferings
were almost incredible.

The democrats at Chicago took advantage of the fact that our soldiers were so confined to denounce the "shameful disregard of the administraton to its duty, in respect to our fellow-citizens who are now and long have been prisoners of war, in a suffering condition, as deserving the severest reprobation, on the score alike of public interest and common humanity."

Great suffering was, undoubtedly, experienced by the prisoners on both sides, in consequence of the interruption of the cartel. The president was, technically, as the head of the government, held responsible for the cruel detention and confinement of prisoners, but neither he nor the members of the administration, except the secretary of war and the lieutenant-general, were then aware that the exchange had, by the authority of these two officials, ceased.

The democratic convention, in its resolutions, arraigned the administration as violently as the radicals through Wade and Winter Davis, for its usurpation and its exercise of extraordinary and dangerous powers not granted by the constitution; also for the subversion of civil by military law in States not in insurrection; for arbitrary military arrests, imprisonment, trial, and sentence of American citizens in States where civil law existed in full force; for the suppression of freedom of speech and of the press; for disregard of State's rights; for the imposition of test oaths, etc., etc.

Although there had been some recent improvement in military operations to lighten the almost insupportable load which had depressed the Union men through the summer, the reverses actually encouraged and animated the democrats while electing their delegates. The convention thus chosen declared that "after four years of failure to restore the Union by the experiment of war, humanity, liberty, and the public welfare demanded that immediate efforts be made for a cessation of hostilities."

Availing themselves of every difficulty that beset the government,—of the financial embarrassment, military stagnation, opposition to the draft and calls for more troops, the radical hostility to the president for what was called usurpation, and the general depression that prevailed and was a growing discouragement after Grant's arrival and nonaction near Richmond,— the democrats made the clamor for peace the watch-cry at their party gatherings during the summer. The Chicago resolutions were responsive to and in coöperation with this and with the cunningly devised peace schemes which had captivated Greeley and others who, if not in full harmony with the radicals, had become tired of the war which they themselves had invoked, and, without any definite ideas of their own how to bring it to a close, were dissatisfied with the president and wanted another candidate. In fact, the whole platform of principles, though not destitute of patriotic professions, was factious, denunciatory of the administration, and unjust to the government involved in war for the national life. But the Chicago proceedings, although sent out with bluster and bravado, fell coldly upon the public ear. They were not what the Union men had expected. It was soon evident that the convention had, under the spur and pressure of heated partisanship, committed an error, and that it would have been well to have listened to the wiser and more considerate views of the moderate and conservative members. But the conservatives lacked resolution,—courage to face and resist the violent and reckless, and proclaim and enforce a different and more statesman-like course.

General McClellan, whom the democrats nominated as their candidate for president, had the sagacity to see that the party managers at Chicago had been carried away by the vituperative harangues and inflammatory declamations of superficial and disunion speakers; he nevertheless accepted the nomination. In his letter of acceptance, however, he disavowed and virtually repudiated the platform of the convention, to the great disgust of the peace democrats, who opposed the administration and made it a point to declare "the war a failure," and insisted on the "immediate cessation of hostilities." He said to his friends in this letter: "The Union was originally formed by the exercise of a spirit of conciliation and compromise. To restore and preserve it, the same spirit must prevail in our councils and in the hearts of the people. The reëstablishment of the Union in all its integrity is and must continue to be the indispensable condition in any settlement. . . . The Union is the one condition of peace. . . . When any State is willing to return to the Union it should be received at once, with a full guarantee of all its constitutional rights. If a frank, earnest, and persistent effort to obtain these objects should fail, the responsibility for ulterior consequences will fall upon those who remain in arms against the Union; but the Union must be preserved at all hazards. . . . I would hail with unbounded joy the permanent restoration of peace on the basis of the Union under the constitution without the effusion of another drop of blood; but no peace can be permanent without union."

These views and opinions were so much in accord with those of President Lincoln—it was so manifest that General McClellan, away from Chicago and the factious and party influences there dominant, had arrived at the same conclusion as the president in regard to conciliation and the restoration of the Union—that the extremists of the party were dissatisfied, and some of them were for taking immediate steps for another candidate. Before his letter appeared a perceptible change had taken place in the public mind. The Chicago resolutions had fallen heavy on every man of patriotic sentiments who read them; the democrats, especially those who had opposed secession and were for sustaining the government, could not accept or acquiesce in the peace programme. Regardless of mere party organization, they had, in 1861, rallied to uphold the flag when it was assailed at Sumter, in conformity with their Union principles and from a high sense of duty. The war experience and the condition of affairs in 1864 had led them to anticipate that such a course would be marked out and adopted at Chicago as would enable them to become reconciled with their former democratic associates in reorganizing the party and supporting its candidates, but the resolutions and the doctrines avowed repelled them.

President Lincoln, had, with a good deal of hesitation, relieved General McClellan from the command of the army of the Potomac in November, 1862. Although the general had decided opponents in the war department, and there were military officers opposed to him, yet no one was more popular in that army or had more fully the confidence of the soldiers than the general in command. In removing him, which was with reluctance, the president gratified a large portion of the republican citizens; but there were some who, like the democrats, condemned the removal as a mistake that was almost inexcusable. Not without reason had the general been censured for dilatory movements, but his tardy operations were now contrasted with the immobility of Grant, who, with a much larger force, was wasting the summer of 1864 on the same ground that McClellan had occupied in 1862, without making further advance. Earnest and distinguished democrats, and some republicans in whom he had confidence, now advised and urged upon the president the reinstatement of McClellan. They gave as a reason that he was a man of intelligence and culture superior to Grant's, and that this movement would annihilate the peace party, utterly defeat the democrats, and break down the democratic organization. The president had yielded to Stanton and Halleck in 1862, who pressed the general's displacement while in command of the army of the Potomac before Richmond. Having reinstated him after Pope's defeat, with Halleck's concurrence, the president was slow in listening a second time to the earnest and persistent demand of the war department and head-quarters that he should dismiss McClellan for alleged neglect and remissness following the battle of Antietam. But added to the representations of the war department was the dilatory conduct of the general, whose vacillating and perverse course was such that the president was forced to the conclusion that it was a duty to relieve him. This he finally did, deliberately and on conviction, in 1862. He was not disposed to reverse the act in 1864, and again reinstate that officer,—certainly not on mere party grounds and for merely party purposes. In these conclusions the Union element of the country was clearly with the president. There had been, moreover, a feeling on the part of some that McClellan was not sufficiently earnest in prosecuting the war, and his nomination by the peace democrats for a time intensified that feeling.

With the Chicago clamor for peace came tidings of the triumphant achievements of Farragut at Mobile, and Sherman at Atlanta. These tidings revived at once, as if by an electric charm, the previously drooping spirits of the people. Those democrats who from the first had opposed secession and supported the war, and the republicans who were untainted with radicalism, had been the strength of the government in the great conflict from

1861, and they were now again consolidated. The radical faction, which had been fierce, insolent, and overbearing in Congress, was found to be weak with the people; and the vituperative assaults upon the president, such as the arrogant and denunciatory protest of Wade and Winter Davis, were almost universally condemned. Even their fellow congressmen who had egged them on fell away as the country was aroused, withheld their names, and shrank from association with those presuming protestants against Lincoln and his policy. Wade's appointments to address the people of Ohio in the political campaign then progressing were canceled by the state committee, and Davis failed to secure even a renomination from the republicans of his own district in Baltimore. The discountenance of these extremists, who, in the plenitude of their party management and power in Washington, had deemed themselves irresistible, and with bold front, had denounced the conciliatory measures of the executive and his policy of reconstruction, instead of injuring President Lincoln actually inspired confidence in his administration, and contributed to bring again almost the whole of the war supporters into cordial unity. It became apparent that Congress, or the radical faction, was not, as it assumed, the embodiment or the correct exponent of the popular sentiment of the country; that though the leaders might, by secret operations and party machinery, so discipline a majority of that body as to procure a legislative sanction of their proscriptive and intolerant views, the hearts and feelings of the nation were not with them in their exclusive schemes, which were really disunion and sectional, but with the president in his endeavors to promote tranquillity, nationality, reconstruction and a restoration of the Union.

Whatever disappointment was experienced in consequence of Grant's inaction before Richmond, it was measurably unrelieved by the military and naval successes in the Southwest.

On the 29th of August, the day on which the Chicago convention assembled, information was received, through the rebel lines, that Fort Morgan, which guarded the entrance to the bay of Mobile, had surrendered. This intelligence, after a summer of inaction of the great army on the James, was inspiring and invigorating. It cheered the president and the whole administration; the navy department was encouraged to renew efforts, long previously made, to close the port of Wilmington by capturing the forts at the mouth of Cape Fear River. Through this channel, which it was difficult to blockade, the rebels had received their principal supplies; and now that the navy had obtained possession of the forts, and our squadron was in Mobile Bay, Wilmington remained the only important port where blockade running was in the least successful. To close that port, and thus terminate the intercourse of the rebels with the outer world, would be like severing the jugular vein in the human system. Richmond and the whole insurrectionary region, which, even before Grant reached the James, was in an exhausted and suffering condition, could not, if deprived of foreign aid and succor, long hold out against the Union arms. It was in view of these circumstances, and of the almost total immobility of the armies of the Potomac and the James, that in the latter part of the summer, while the military seemed waiting events and the administration and country also were greatly depressed, I proposed that the army should send a force to coöperate with the navy against Forts Fisher and Caswell, at the mouth of Cape Fear River. The secretary of war and General Halleck had on previous occasions seemed indifferent, if not actually opposed, to the movement. But the changed condition of things in the Gulf and the Southwest, and the fact that the large military force on the James was doing so little, favored the project. The president earnestly sanctioned it, and thought the war department might now come into it, and was himself ready to make the expedition an administration measure. General Grant, he thought, would be disposed to avail himself of the opportunity to employ a portion of his large force in a work that would weaken the enemy and strengthen his own operations against the rebel capital.

The war department, after Grant was made lieutenant-general and had taken command of the armies in the field, seemed willing to devolve upon him the responsibility as well as the honors of the campaign, and in one or two interviews signified a willingness to refer the whole subject, so far as the military were con-

cerned, to that officer, with the single exception, by the secretary
of war, that General Q. A. Gillmore should be designated to
command the military forces, should the expedition be ordered.
To this there was on the part of the president and the navy no
objection, and to facilitate the movement the assistant secretary
of the navy, Mr. Fox, whose zeal and efforts in the project were
earnest and devoted, and General Gillmore, designated by the
war department, went to the front on the 31st of August to
lay the subject before General Grant and enlist him in its favor.
In this they found no difficulty; for, although the general himself
had little originality, was barren of resources and by no means
fertile in strategy, he possessed, in general, good judgment in
passing on the plans of others, was always willing to avail himself
of valuable suggestions, and in this instance was ready to adopt
the plan and aid in carrying it out. It is singular that the general-
in-chief should have lain three months in front of the rebel
capital without any attempt or thought of cutting off its only
channel of supplies from abroad, but, as already stated, he relied
on others to make suggestions. He was prompt to acquiesce in
this one, and, as his friend Admiral Porter, who knew him well,
remarks, was willing also to appropriate to himself the credit
of the expedition. It was characteristic. It was Admiral Foote
who proposed the capture of Forts Henry and Donelson, in the
winter of 1862; it was Sherman and Porter who projected the
many schemes at Vicksburg and vicinity, except the last successful demonstration, which originated with Farragut, who, in
1863, when lying between Grand Gulf and Vicksburg, sent his
marine officer, Captain, now Major, John L. Broome, and Pay-
master Meredith, of the Hartford, across the peninsula at Vicksburg, and advised that the army should come below and make
its advance, instead of wasting its strength and that of the navy
above, on the Yazoo; it was the president and the navy department that, in 1864, suggested to him the capture of Cape Fear
and the port of Wilmington, as an important point, not only for
the blockade, but in the operations against Richmond. It is
proper the facts should be stated, for the expedition against
Fort Fisher was a subject of consultation at Washington, and
had the sanction and approval of the president before it was

communicated to or known by General Grant. No credit, however, is given by the histories of the period to the administration
or the navy, which projected it and devoted months of incessant
labor and a large expenditure to that great object. The honors
won were awarded to General Grant, who complacently received
them.

Horace Greeley, in his American Conflict, a valuable work in
many respects, and which he intended should be truthful, but
which exhibits at times the party prejudices and personal bias
of the author, introduces the subject of the expedition and capture of Fort Fisher as follows: "To close it [the port of Wilming-
ton], therefore, became at length synonymous with barring all
direct and nearly all commercial intercourse between the Confederacy and the non-belligerent world. Early in the autumn of
1864, General Grant proposed to General Butler the dispatch of
Brigadier-Generals Weitzel and Graham to reconnoitre Fort
Fisher, the main defense of the sea-approaches to Wilmington, to
determine its strength, preparatory to a combined attack."

The impression that General Grant planned the expedition to
capture Fort Fisher and the other defenses of Wilmington, and
close the port, was prevalent when the History of the American
Conflict was written. Grant did consult Butler, and Weitzel and
Graham were sent to reconnoitre, but this was after the navy
department had suggested it. Mr. Greeley was evidently confirmed
in his impression, if he did not derive it from the official report
of the lieutenant-general, who, without openly assuming the
credit, certainly did not repel it.

It was a knowledge of this erroneous impression which gave
dissatisfaction to naval men who were cognizant of the facts,
and led Rear-Admiral Porter, who was in command, to write to
me from his "Flag Ship Malvern, Cape Fear River," January
24, 1865: "To the navy department alone is the country indebted
for the capture of this rebel stronghold; for had it not been
for your perseverence in keeping the fleet here, and your constant
propositions made to the army, nothing would have been done.
As it was, after the proposition had been received and General
Grant promised that the troops should be sent, it was not done
until General Butler consented to let the matter go on, and when

he hoped to reap some little credit from the explosion of the powder-boat. Now the country gives General Grant the credit of inaugurating the expedition, when on both occasions he permitted it to go properly provided. In the first place it had neither head nor tail, so far as the army was concerned. . . .

"Now that the most important port on the coast has been gained, as usual you will hear of but little that the navy did, and no doubt efforts will be made again to show that the work was 'not substantially injured as a defensive work.' To General Grant, who is always willing to take the credit when anything is done, and equally ready to lay the blame of the failure on the navy when a failure takes place, I feel under no obligations for receiving and allowing a report to be spread from his head-quarters that there were three days when the navy might have operated and did not. He knows as much about it as he did when he wrote to me, saying 'the only way in which the place could be taken was by running the ships past the batteries,' showing, evidently, that he had not studied the hydrography of Cape Fear River, and did not know the virtue there was in our wooden walls when they went in for a fair stand-up fight. . . . I have served with the lieutenant-general before, when I never worked so hard in my life to make a man succeed as I did for him. You will scarcely notice in his reports that the navy did him any service, when without the help it has given him, all the way through, he would never have been lieutenant-general. He wants magnanimity, like most officers of the army, and is so avaricious as regards fame that he will never, if he can help it, do justice to our department.

"When the rebels write the history of this war, then, and only then, will the country be made to feel what the navy has done. . . . His course proves to me that he would sacrifice his best friend rather than let any odium fall upon Lieutenant-General Grant. He will take to himself all the credit of this move, now that it is successful, when he deserves all the blame for the first failure. . . .

"I remain, respectfully and sincerely,
"Your obedient servant,
"DAVID D. PORTER."

These are the freely and frankly expressed opinions of the chief naval officer in the Fort Fisher expedition, written in the private and unreserved confidence of an officer in command to the secretary under whom he acted and who was entitled to the facts. The publication of this letter from the files of the department was made after the close of my official connection with the navy, and without my knowledge, but the facts stated truthfully express the feelings and opinions of one who long coöperated with General Grant, and understood his character and traits.

By special request of the lieutenant-general, Rear-Admiral Porter had been, on the 22d of September, transferred from the Missouri squadron, where he had served with Grant and coöperated with the army in the capture of Vicksburg, to the North Atlantic squadron, with a view to the command of the expedition against Fort Fisher. This command had been first assigned to Admiral Farragut, on the 5th of September, after the successful mission of Assistant Secretary Fox and General Gillmore to induce General Grant to lend a military force to coöperate with the navy. This was at a period when the tide of affairs, political and military, had taken a favorable turn elsewhere than in the vicinity of Richmond. The proceedings and nomination at Chicago had just been promulgated, Atlanta had fallen, the bay of Mobile and the forts which guarded its entrance were in our possession, and the importance of prompt additional successes and decisive blows was felt by the administration to be necessary. But Admiral Farragut, the great and successful hero of the war, who was selected to command the expedition, had written me on the 27th of August a letter, which I did not receive until after my orders of the 5th of September assigning him to the command of the Fort Fisher expedition, saying his strength was almost exhausted, "but as long as I am able, I am willing to do the bidding of the department to the best of my abilities. I fear, however, my health is giving way. I have now been down in this Gulf and the Caribbean Sea nearly five years out of six, with the exception of the short time at home last fall, and the last six months have been a severe drag upon me, and I want rest if it is to be had."

On receiving this letter, it was felt that further exaction on the energies of this valuable officer ought not to be made; he was therefore relieved from that service, and Rear-Admiral Porter was substituted. The action of the department in giving Porter the command instead of Farragut was much commented upon and never fully understood by the country, which had learned to appreciate the noble qualities of Farragut, and gave him its unstinted confidence. The great admiral always regretted—though on his account I did not—that he had reported his physical sufferings and low state of health before my orders were received or even issued. I have embraced this occasion to make known the facts more in detail than was necessary, perhaps, in relating briefly, not the military, but the political and civil events of Lincoln's administration in the early autumn of 1864. The Fort Fisher expedition was properly an administration rather than a military measure, projected at Washington, not at army head-quarters, and was, after delays, chiefly military, finally successful in January, 1865. Its inception was at a critical and turning period of the political affairs of the country, when the Chicago convention was in session, and the amnesty and reconstruction policy of the administration was opposed and undergoing a severe test. The radical opposition was by no means appeased, but eager and contriving. The party managers of that faction had hopes through the summer that Mr. Chase might yet be selected as a compromise candidate, around whom they and all republicans could rally. That gentleman, after his resignation in June, withdrew from any active participation in the political campaign, which was being prosecuted with vigor while the president was violently assailed by radical friends. So early as May 23d, before the convention met at Baltimore, but when it became certain that Lincoln would be nominated, Chase wrote to a friend that "all under God depends on Grant. So far *he has achieved very little, and that little has cost beyond computation.*"

This was before Mr. Chase resigned, and while he was still secretary. After he left the cabinet, he passed the summer in listless inactivity, or was secretly communing with grumblers. Months wore away without any successful military achievement and with daily increased "cost," though in May he said it was "beyond computation."

In all these trying days not one word of encouragement to
the president or the country came from the ex-secretary, although until the 30th of June he had, but with disappointed
aspirations, been surpassed by no one in zeal and activity for
the public welfare. His abstinence from encouragement and
advice during this period was not from indifference to events
and occurrences that took place. Murmurs of discontent were
uttered, and extracts from his letters and diary evince his
feelings and those of a discontented class with whom he held
communication. In July he wrote that—

"The president pocketed the GREAT BILL [the Winter Davis
bill] providing for the reorganization of the rebel States as loyal
States. He did not venture to veto, and so put it in his pocket. It
[the bill] was a condemnation of his amnesty proclamation, re-
jecting the idea of possible reconstruction with slavery; which
neither the president nor his chief advisers have, in my opinion,
abandoned." He adds that "Mr. Sumner said also that there was
intense indignation against the president on account of his
pocketing the Winter Davis or reconstruction bill."

"I am too earnest, too antislavery, and say too radical to
make him [the president] willing to have me connected with
the administration; just as my opinion that he is not earnest
enough, not antislavery enough, not radical enough, but goes
naturally with those hostile to me rather than with me, makes
me willing and glad to be disconnected from it."

Garfield, Schenck, and Wetmore, he says, "all were bitter
against the timid and almost pro-slavery course of the president."

From the republicans as a party Chase could expect no
nomination,—they had already nominated Lincoln. What had
he to hope for? What could he do? In July he wrote: "Senator
Pomeroy came to breakfast. He says there is great dissatisfaction
with Mr. Lincoln, which has been much excited by the pocketing
of the reorganization bill [Winter Davis bill]. . . . Pomeroy says
he means to go on a buffalo hunt and then to Europe. He
cannot support Lincoln, but won't desert his principles. I am
much of the same sentiments, though not willing now to decide
what duty may demand next fall. Pomeroy remarked that on the

news of my resignation reaching the senate several of the democratic senators came to him and said: 'We'll go with you now
for Chase.' This means nothing but a vehement desire to overthrow the existing administration, *but might mean much* if the
democrats would only cut loose from slavery and go for freedom
and the protection of labor by a national currency. *If they would
do that I would cheerfully go for any man they might nominate.*"

Governor May wrote a letter in reference to a movement in
behalf of Chase for the presidency at a time when he says, "there
was great discouragement and dissatisfaction with Mr. Lincoln's
administration."

Mr. Chase replied on the 31st of August, the Chicago convention having nominated McClellan the day previous: "I am
now a private citizen, and expect to remain such; since my
retirement from the department, I have no connection with political affairs; . . . I see only, as all see, that there is a deplorable lack of harmony, caused chiefly, in my judgment, by the
injudicious course of some of Mr. Lincoln's chief advisers, and
his own action on their advice."

Party movements and the political events of the summer had
not been such as he hoped and expected. The dreams and anticipations of party politicians are often delusive, ending in disappointment. They were so in this instance. Achilles had retired
to his tent, or to the White Mountains, during the summer, and
there learned that his friends and supporters were less in numbers, strength, and influence than he had supposed, and were
also becoming enlisted in the support of Lincoln. On the 14th
day of September, after the nomination of McClellan and the
adoption of suicidal resolutions at Chicago, Chase returned to
Washington, and was kindly welcomed by the president. He
entered in his journal:—

"September 17th. I have seen the president twice since I have
been here. Both times third persons were present, and there was
nothing like private conversation. His manner was cordial, and
so were his words; and I hear nothing but good-will from him.
But he is not at all demonstrative, either in speech or manner.
I feel that I do not know him, and I found no action on what
he says or does. . . . It is my conviction that the cause I love

and the general interests of the country will be best promoted by his reëlection, and I *have resolved* to join my efforts to those of almost the whole body of my friends in securing it. . . . I never desired anything else than his complete success, and never indulged a personal feeling incompatible with absolute fidelity to his administration. . . . But it would be uncandid not to say I felt wronged and hurt by the circumstances which preceded and attended my resignation."

The summer's observation, reflection, and experience, with the determination of "almost the whole body of my friends," convinced Mr. Chase that it was unwise to kick against the pricks; that the current of public opinion after the Chicago convention was becoming irresistible; and that the really substantial and considerate men on whom he depended had yielded to events which they could not control, and concluded that they would support the reëlection of Mr. Lincoln. He therefore, in September, came to the same conclusion, which was confirmed by the genial and cordial manner and the friendly reception by the president. Other attending circumstances reconciled him to the administration. He soon enlisted in the political campaign, made speeches, and contributed to the success of the republican party in the following November.

On the same day that Mr. Chase wrote "I have resolved to join my efforts to those of almost the whole body of my friends" to secure the election of Mr. Lincoln, namely, on the 17th of September, John C. Fremont, the radical or extreme republican candidate, withdrew his name as a presidential candidate, stating that he did so "not to aid in the triumph of Mr. Lincoln, but to do my part toward preventing the election of the democratic candidate. In respect to Mr. Lincoln, I continue to hold exactly the sentiments contained in my letter of acceptance. I consider that his administration has been, politically, militarily, and financially, a failure, and that its necesary continuance is a cause of regret for the country."

In this extract are exposed the radical feelings towards Mr. Lincoln and his administration. The extremists, with their sectional and proscriptive intolerance, were not recognized as correct exponents of the principles and views of the republicans in the autumn of 1864, although at a later period, and under another president, they by caucus machinery and party discipline became the despotic dictators of Congress, and the authors of those sectional measures which prolonged national differences and for years excluded from rightful representation and all participation in the government one third of the States and people of the Union.

On the 23d of September, a few days after Chase had resolved to join his friends and support the president's reëlection, and Fremont, perhaps by concert, at the same time had withdrawn in a dudgeon, Mr. Bates, the attorney-general, and myself left the cabinet meeting together. We stopped for a few moments on the platform of the north portico of the White House, where the postmaster-general, Mr. Blair, soon joined us, and as he did so remarked, "I suppose you gentlemen are aware I am no longer a member of the cabinet." So far from being aware of this it was a surprise to us both. As the meeting, where we had only pleasant conversation on miscellaneous topics, had just adjourned, without any allusion to the subject, we were incredulous until Mr. Blair repeated that he had resigned.

The sudden and unexpected retirement of a member of the administration would at any time create a sensation in the country, and especially excite his colleagues and associates in the government; this wholly unanticipated and unexplained step astounded us. Each inquired what it meant, what was the cause, and how long the subject had been under consideration. There had been grumbling, complaints, intrigues, often unjust, as there always will be, against members of every cabinet. Mr. Blair, as well as others, had been the subject of such assaults. Probably no member of the cabinet had greater influence with the president on important questions, especially those of a military character, than Mr. Blair. Politically, he had little sympathy with or respect for the radicals, and did not conceal his opposition to their ultra ideas, which would, if carried out, end in sectionalism, exclusion, and, ultimately, in separation. On the subject of amnesty and reconstruction he and the president agreed, and those subjects were, in the pending political campaign, to be put to a test. Why then this break? It was from no dissatisfaction on the part of either the president or the postmaster-general. In answer to an inquiry how long the subject of his resignation had been meditated, he replied that we were as well enlightened on that point as he was.

Mr. Blair called at my house that evening, and read the correspondence which had passed between the president and himself. The whole proceeding had been in the most amicable spirit and with the utmost harmony of feeling and friendly understanding on the part of both. Thinking that parties had assumed such shape, personally and politically, that the president might, in the course of events, deem it expedient and politic to modify or change his cabinet, or a portion of it, and yet feel a delicacy in taking such a step, Blair had repeatedly said that if his resignation would conduce to pacification or be a relief, the president had only to signify the fact and the office of postmaster-general was at his disposal. No farther interchange of sentiments between them had ever taken place, nor anything which could be construed into an intimation of a purpose to make a change, with perhaps the single exception of what he at the time supposed were casual remarks, the preceding day, when Fremont's letter declining to be a candidate was discussed and criticised. The president, in that conversation, said that Fremont, when getting out of the way, had stated "the administration was a failure, politically, militarily, and financially"; this, the president remarked, included, he supposed, the secretaries of state, treasury, and war, and the postmaster-general, and he thought the interior also, but not the secretary of the navy or the attorney-general.

With this exception, Mr. Blair said he had received no intimation from the president that his retirement was wanted until he found upon his table, when he came in that morning from Silver Spring, the following letter:

EXECUTIVE MANSION, WASHINGTON, ⎫
September 23, 1864.   ⎭

HON. MONTGOMERY BLAIR:

MY DEAR SIR, — You have generously said to me more than once that whenever your resignation could be a relief to me it was at my disposal. The time has come. You very well know that this proceeds from no dissatisfaction with you, personally

or officially. Your uniform kindness has been unsurpassed by
that of any friend; and while it is true that the war does not
so greatly add to the difficulties of your department as to
those of some others, it is yet much to say, as I most truly
can, that in the three years and a half during which you have
administered the general post-office, I remember no single
complaint against you in connection therewith.

Yours as ever,
ABRAHAM LINCOLN.

The resignation was promptly written, and handed to the
president personally, who received it with many expressions
of kind regard and friendship.

In answer to a question as to the immediate cause which led
to this step, for there must be a reason for it,—Blair said it certainly was not from any disagreement between the president and
himself, as I would see by the letter, but he had no doubt his
retirement was peace-offering to Fremont and the radicals. He
reminded me that the president, if somewhat peculiar, was also
sagacious, and that he comprehended the true condition of affairs; that his own retirement was all right, and would eventuate
well; that something was needed to propitiate Fremont and
furnish the radicals an excuse in their retreat; that they had, in
their wild crusade against the South, mounted a high horse
which they found unmanageable, and they required help to dis-
mount; that the tide of public sentiment for the reëlection of the
president was irresistible; and that the radicals and all discontented republicans would now come in to the support of Lincoln,
who would certainly be elected and successful in his policy.

In a conversation with the president, subsequently, he not
only spoke of reconciling the Fremont element, but said Mr.
Chase had many friends who felt grieved that he should have
left the cabinet, and left alone. There had been for a year a bitter
feud between Chase and the Blairs, growing out of alleged abuse
and misrepresentation of General Blair by certain of the treasury
agents, in which the secretary of the treasury took part with
his subordinates, and the postmaster-general, very naturally, defended his brother, who he believed was unjustly treated. It is
not necessary here to enter into the details of that quarrel, more

personal than political, though for a time it partook, with some, of a partisan character. The president regretted the feud, but avoided any committal to either party. The secretary of the treasury, who at that time had high aspirations, was not satisfied with neutrality, but thought that in not sustaining him the president supported the Blairs.

This was also one of the charges made by the friends of the secretary in Congress, and by the treasury officials generally, who insisted that the retention of General Blair in a high position in the army, his brother, the postmaster-general, in the cabinet, and Commodore Lee, a brother-in-law, in command of the North Atlantic squadron, while Mr. Chase, with whom they had a personal quarrel, left the cabinet, was in effect a discrimination in favor of the Blairs.

As indicative of the feeling of Mr. Chase himself, and that the subject, which some strove to make political and general, may be fully understood, one or two brief extracts from letters of Mr. Chase may be introduced. He wrote to Jay Cooke on the 5th of May:—

"I seldom consult personal considerations in my public conduct, and so suppressed my inclination to resign my office and denounce the conspiracy of which the Blairs are the most visible embodiments."

The next day, the 6th of May, he wrote to Colonel R. C. Parsons:—

"Of Blair's outrageous speech and its apparent, though I am sure not intended, indorsement by Mr. Lincoln, nothing can change the character of the Blair-Lincoln transaction so far as the public is concerned."

On the 10th of May he writes:—

"I use as much philosophy as I can in relation to the Blairs . . . and the apparent indifference to it all of Mr. Lincoln, who, though he disclaims all sympathy with them in their speech and action, does nothing to arrest either."

May 19th he writes:—

"The convention [at Baltimore, in June] will not be regarded as a Union convention, but simply as a Blair-Lincoln convention, by a great body of citizens whose support is essential to success."

To Alfred P. Stone he says, on the 23d of May:—

"I have not written a word to Ohio, I believe, on the villainous, malignant, and lying assault of the Blairs—for the congressional general was only the mouth-piece of the trio—and its apparent indorsement by Mr. Lincoln."

These extracts from his writings are quoted as exhibiting the animus, the intense personal animosity, that existed and for months had been nursed and cherished by Mr. Chase and his friends. It was probably not less intense on the part of those whom he denounced. The president had been anxious, even while beset with public affairs, to allay this controversy in his political family, and to unite all, indeed, who were opposed to secession.

For some time there had also been an estrangement between the postmaster-general and the secretary of war, which seemed connected with the Chase and Blair controversy. This difference or enmity had been not only unpleasant but exceedingly annoying and distressing to the president. The estrangement was mysteriously brought on by some one who had an object in producing alienation, and was of such a character that it could not be reconciled or removed. The facts were that at an early period of the administration, in the spring of 1861, Edwin M. Stanton was pressed by Mr. Seward for the office of attorney for the District of Colombia. The attorney-general, Mr. Bates, was very earnest for General Carrington. Other members of the cabinet abstained from interference, until the president, tired of delay, requested the opinion of each. Mr. Blair, who, being a resident in Washington, knew all the competitors, personally and professionally, was specially asked his opinion. Thus called upon, Mr. Blair spoke of Mr. Stanton as possessing superior legal ability, and as occupying a higher standing at the bar, but stated a fact within his personal knowledge which affected the integrity of that gentleman. This was decisive against Mr. Stanton. Within less than a year, however, on the retirement of Mr. Cameron, Mr. Seward succeeded, by skillfull management assisted by adventitious circumstances, in securing the position about to be made vacant for his friend and confidant, Mr. Stanton, the unsuccessful candidate for district attorney. It has been represented by Mr. Chase and Mr. Cameron respectively, and perhaps

believed by each, that he procured the selection of Stanton to be
secretary of war. Mr. Stanton himself knew otherwise, and so
did Mr. Seward. The latter, however, satisfied with his success in
bringing his friend and confidant into the cabinet, was willing
that the others should assume credit for what he had accomplished. The president took no part in those rivalries and
pretensions, nor in the differences between Stanton and Blair
at a later period. In administering the government, however, he
was necessarily brought into close official and personal intimacy
with Mr. Stanton on all military questions, yet he seldom failed
to consult and he relied greatly on the intelligence, experience,
and judgment of Mr. Blair, who had received a military education, had been an army officer, and was more familiar with and
better understood the *personnel* of the service than the secretary
of war or any of his colleagues. Mr. Stanton himself took much
the same view as the president, and for a year or two deferred
much to the opinions and judgment of Mr. Blair, who was
almost daily at the war office, consulting and advising in regard to
military operations. About the close of the year 1863, it was noticed that Mr. Stanton became reticent and uncommunicative
towards the postmaster-general. This coolness grew so marked that
Blair demanded an explanation. Stanton said he had been informed that Blair had made statements injurious to his character. Blair, understanding to what he alluded, replied that
he had volunteered no statement, but when called upon by the
president, on a certain occasion, he had communicated, in the
frankness and confidence of cabinet consultation, as was his
duty, certain facts which Stanton knew to be true. Without
inquiring who had betrayed confidence, Blair said he had stated
what Stanton knew to be a fact. This terminated all friendly intercourse. Neither ever after visited the other, or exchanged
civilities. Whenever the president desired the views of either, he
was compelled to get their opinions separately, or in general
cabinet consultations. This political domestic controversy, which
it was impossible to reconcile, had added to the other troubles
of the president.

Mr. Blair comprehended all these embarrassments, personal
and political, that environed Mr. Lincoln, not only in putting

down the rebellion, but in quelling differences in the administration and in overcoming the radical faction that persistently opposed his reëlection; as well as the wretched intrigues which sought to place the president on a level with Fremont, and, by antagonizing the two, compel him to decline for a more acceptable and more radical candidate, who would carry into effect the radical scheme of putting the States of the South under ban, and by federal power disfranchise and degrade the whites, and enfranchise the blacks, reducing the one and elevating the other to a condition of legal and social equality. These factious intrigues, which had been active through 1864, failed in their purpose. The unpatriotic action of the Chicago convention largely contributed to bring into harmonious action every element of the republican party, but something seemed wanting as an excuse or reason for radical support of Mr. Lincoln, after the violent denunciations which had been uttered. As Mr. Blair, who, besides his personal differences with Chase and Stanton, was emphatic and pronounced against the aggressive, exclusive, and sectional policy of the radicals, had generously proposed to the president that he would resign whenever his doing so would relieve the president, his resignation, so unselfishly tendered, was requested. When it took place, his retirement was considered a peace-offering which would close up differences, contribute to insure success in the election, and put an end to the proscriptive intolerance and sectional exclusion of the radical leaders.

Such was the result in the election, and such would also have been the result in the matter of restoration and reconstruction but for the assassination of President Lincoln, after his second inauguration, and just as the rectitude of his benignant policy was beginning to be appreciated.